Echoes of
Morrison, Wisconsin

ECHOES OF MORRISON, WISCONSIN

True Stories from the Pioneer Era

By Zelo Anderson

Pleasant View Publishing

Published by Pleasant View Publishing
De Pere, Wisconsin

ISBN: 979-8-9855864-3-5
First Edition: 2025

For Don & Nancy, my loving parents.

TABLE OF CONTENTS

Introduction 1
The Branch River & The Boiling Body 4
Madman Maloney & Other Trials of Insanity 7
The Founder & Electric Soap 12
A Land Before Morrison 19
The Union Hotel, Social Security, & the Green Bay Packers 25
Wayside's Sore Winners 30
Quarrels Over Quarantine 34
Dark & Stormy Nights 39
War 43
Loyal – Or Not? 49
Drama 54
Long, Lost Letters & Very Vulgar Phone Calls 58
Painful Progress 63
Say Cheese... & Calamity 72
Murder 76
Haunted 80
Let's Have a Drink 85
Scorned Love & Scandals 90
Chaos, Crime, & Comedy 97
The Final Curtain 105
End of an Era 121

"Perhaps the echoes of people we once loved still linger in the places we frequented with them…and that is why we go back. Not so much to remember them as to feel them…"
— Ranata Suzuki

Introduction

On June 11, 1961, people throughout the Town of Morrison, a small unincorporated community in Brown County, Wisconsin, gathered to dedicate a beautiful new public space: Way-Morr Park. It was a moment of pride, marking not just a place for future generations to gather, but a quiet nod to the community's long past.

In the days leading up to the grand opening, a memorial stone was placed there. This tribute still rests atop a hill in the park. Its inscription reads: "Dedicated to the memory of the pioneers who settled this area."

This silent monument honors those who came before us.

Yet, like much of local history, that stone is often passed by without a second thought. Many who head to Morrison's sprawling 32-acre park never stop to look at it. Most don't even know it exists. And, all too often, visitors rush toward the playground, a park shelter, or the serene resting spots beyond, without pausing to reflect.

But the stories within this book invite you to pause, reflect, and to look back—specifically at the first 100 years of the Town of Morrison, it's "pioneer era" from 1855 to 1955—and discover the struggles, mishaps, accomplishments, odd adventures, and resilience of its earliest residents.

This covers all corners of the Town of Morrison, including its "hamlets" of Morrison, Wayside, and Lark (which are essentially three small subsections of an already tiny town).

It must be noted, too, that the Town of Morrison has marked milestone anniversaries—such as its 150th anniversary in 2005—by having volunteers put together commemorative history booklets. Those publications have done a tremendous job of giving a summary of businesses and local landmarks and telling a broad chronological story of the town's history. We are grateful those books exist and praise the work of all who made them possible.

But this book takes a different approach. It goes far deeper into the day-to-day world and untold stories from Morrison's earliest era. Research of more than 400 newspaper articles from Morrison's pioneer days helped craft these true stories. Some are humorous and heartwarming. Others are unusual, tragic, and heartbreaking.

While reading through this collection, you may be surprised to find that history, even in a tiny place like Morrison, Wisconsin, is often more entertaining than you imagined.

It's sometimes more painful, too.

You might also find that digging into history can be uncomfortable—and, with that, here's a word of caution that the stories ahead may not be appropriate for younger audiences (or older readers who prefer that their stories remain as quaint and inviting as the hillsides of Way-Morr Park).

The truth is, people suffered greatly in the pioneer days, and this book doesn't shy from that reality. People are also complicated, and their stories can be difficult and unpleasant. Sharing these tales honestly isn't meant to sensationalize hardship, drudge up shame or heartache, or point fingers—it's meant to acknowledge the realities of our past and honor those who lived it with authentic, truthful reflection.

So, enjoy this moment to pause and reflect. Perhaps you'll find the echoes of yesterday are more than distant memories. They are a timeless heartbeat that connects us… and carries us forward.

The Branch River & The Boiling Body

In August 1885, two boys were enjoying a fishing and swimming trip in Morrison's Branch River when their peaceful day took a horrifying turn. Near the riverbank bushes, they stumbled upon a man boiling a human body in a large kettle. Whether it was the skeleton of a man or woman was unclear.

The head was missing from the body.

Amid buzzing insects, drifting birds, and the sight of steam swirling around the corpse, the terrified boys ran for their lives. They sought refuge with neighbors, recounting their frightening discovery. News spread quickly through the quiet Town of Morrison, leaving everyone stunned.

The man responsible was said to be Thomas Burke, a well-regarded figure in the community. The idea that he was boiling a headless human carcass by the river was nauseating and unthinkable. Two nearby cemeteries, one in Morrison and one in nearby Maple Grove, were searched for signs of grave tampering, but none were found. The question remained: what was Burke doing with this body, and where did it come from?

Determined to uncover the truth, Town Chairman D. H. Martin confronted Burke. One can only imagine Martin's thoughts as he prepared to face the man accused of such a grotesque act.

4

Surprisingly, Burke did not deny the accusation. Instead, he calmly claimed he had purchased the body from a Chicago medical college for $80. The purchase was to aid in his medical studies, he said. At the time, such purchases were unusual but not unheard of, as plastic and plaster skeletons were obviously decades away from becoming common. Burke said he spent three days boiling the body on his father's farm to prepare it as a teaching and learning tool. He insisted he had done nothing illegal. To further support this story, he eventually furnished proof of his purchase.

With no evidence of grave robbing and this documentation to support his claims, the community was satisfied. No charges were filed.

This brought an end to an odd saga in Morrison, but it was just the beginning of a long and notable career for Thomas Burke.

Two years later, in 1887, Burke graduated from Rush Medical College in Chicago. He returned to his hometown of Wayside, where he practiced medicine for more than thirty years. Dr. Burke became a pillar of the Morrison community, answering calls at all hours and providing care for the sick and injured.

Known as a highly-skilled physician, he also served as a schoolteacher, statesman, devout church member, and local advisor. He was instrumental in founding the Wayside State Bank, serving as its president for a decade. Burke's dedication to his community earned him widespread admiration.

He married Jessie Joyce in 1893, and together they raised six children. Despite his many accomplishments, it is said that his family was his greatest joy.

The Branch River, meanwhile, remained an idyllic place for fishing and fun for future generations. But it did have its share of other dark moments, too.

In July 1939, a 15-year-old girl drowned while trying to save her younger brother, who had fallen off an inner tube. Her body was recovered two hours later. In 1955, during Morrison's centennial year, a 67-year-old woman drowned near her home. The eternal riddle of why these losses transpired remains confounding.

As for Dr. Burke, following years of noble service, he died in 1921 at the age of 65 after a two-month illness, and his loss was deeply felt. In stark contrast to the skeleton controversy that once required an in-depth explanation, very little needed to be said on the day Dr. Burke was laid to rest, according to close friend and neighbor, Judge N. J. Monahan.

"The death of Dr. Burke [is a] blow not only to his community and the surrounding county, but the entire state. He was a good honest doctor who was anxious and willing to serve at all times... So respected and admired was he by his fellowmen, that no word of praise is needed at his death, for his life speaks for itself."

Dr. Burke was buried near a Maple Grove church in what is said to be one of the largest funerals ever held in the Morrison region at the time.

Flags were set at half-mast, and businesses suspended their activities during the morning of the service, to pay respect.

Madman Maloney & Other Trials of Insanity

A train roared through rural Wisconsin in November 1878. The sun was nearly set, its last light slipping through rustling leaves. In this fading glow, the train rumbled toward the Northern State Hospital for the Insane near Oshkosh.

This institution, built in 1871, housed up to 650 people. John Maloney, a respected Morrison farmer, had no intention of becoming its latest occupant.

But local authorities disagreed.

Doctors deemed Maloney "crazy as a bedbug," and his commitment was arranged. But north of Wrightstown, the "bedbug" took flight. Without warning, he leapt from the moving train meant to deliver him to the asylum.

Maloney's escape wasn't his first. Earlier that month, after showing troubling behavior, he was taken to Green Bay for evaluation. Authorities hoped he would improve—rehabilitation was always the goal—but fate had other plans. Within days, Maloney quietly slipped away and returned to his farm in Morrison.

His condition worsened. He allegedly became violent toward his family, forcing his neighbors to intervene. Three men attempted to bring him back to Green Bay, but Maloney's incredible strength made it impossible. The group had no choice but to call police to help finish bringing him into town.

Brought before a judge once again, Maloney was declared insane and ordered to Oshkosh. A deputy sheriff was assigned to escort him by train on November 14.

Maloney, however, was not only strong; he was cunning. Complaining about smoke in the front cars, he maneuvered to the rear. Then, in a flash, he hurled himself from the moving train into the autumn darkness.

The train screeched to a halt. Men with lanterns fanned out, searching. *Nothing.* The sheriff wired for reinforcements in Wrightstown while Maloney, unseen, doubled back south along the tracks.

Sadly, Maloney's leap to freedom set off a frantic manhunt that ended in a wild—and deadly—farmyard brawl, earning him the infamous nickname "Maloney the Madman" in local headlines.

The exact cause of Maloney's alleged breakdown remains unclear. In his era, patients were often diagnosed with conditions like mania (marked by delusions and overactivity), dementia (then broadly applied to intellectual decline, including brain injuries), or melancholia (characterized by deep depression and irrational fears).

Others in Morrison's pioneer era also had their "sanity" judged in a courtroom.

In 1899, a different Morrison farmer was brought before a judge and also declared insane. Just a year earlier, he had been known as one of the best farmers in the area. What led to his decline is unclear, but according to reports, he became convinced he was being persecuted by unknown enemies, his thoughts consumed by fear. After being sentenced, he was escorted to the same Northern State Hospital that Maloney had avoided by train escape a decade earlier.

That same year, yet another man from Morrison was also brought before a judge, though he was ruled sane and released to family in Milwaukee.

In 1905, after a smallpox quarantine was lifted at the Winnebago institution, another Morrison woman, age 29 years old, was deemed insane and committed there. This came after a request from her father that she be examined by two doctors.

Perhaps the strangest case occurred in 1895, when a Morrison man suspected of insanity rode his horse into Wrightstown, acting erratically. He was taken to the county jail, where his behavior only worsened. Through the night, he allegedly let out wild ravings, barking like a dog. He also said he got bit by one, though no one could find any bite marks to support his claims. The man also shouted about religion and tore apart his bedsheets before getting into a fight with the turnkey, striking him above the eye. Whether he was ultimately committed remains unknown.

While some of these actions may seem a bit amusing now that enough time has passed, it's important to remember that these were real people who shouldered profound burdens in their time. Day after day, their work was far more physically demanding than most of us will experience in a lifetime. On top of that, many faced emotional and mental struggles that we may not easily relate to. The pioneers were settling into a strange and unfamiliar place, often far from their native states—or even countries. There were predators in the woods, terrible illnesses and diseases circulating, and the losses and horrors of the Civil War were still fresh in people's minds. And that's not counting the more common struggles we better relate to, including difficulties with romance, finances, careers, and the shifting dynamics of friends and family.

These hardships simply became too much for some to bear, regardless of age. One harrowing example took place in 1872, when an 84-year-old man in Morrison died after cutting his own throat. His story was, unfortunately, not the only example of this somber fate for the town's earliest residents.

We introduce these uncomfortable facts solely to help convey the weight of the struggles from this era.

These painful moments from long ago, and the stark reality of an institution like the Northern State Hospital (now the Winnebago Mental Health Institute), are an important reminder to all of us—years and decades and even centuries afterward—that complex mental conditions and personal hardship persist in all eras and in all settings of human existence.

The early Town of Morrison was no exception, where the fragilities of mental health could also affect the lives of anyone—a neighbor, a friend, or even a respected farmer like John Maloney.

Returning now to 1878, after Maloney jumped off the train and vanished into darkness, his escape wouldn't last long.

Eventually, he stumbled onto a farm, with reports differing in who lived there, but the most reliable accounts attribute it to a Zeitlow family.

What followed was pure chaos. Maloney stormed into the house, catching the family confused and off guard. He then started attacking Mrs. Zeitlow, dragging her outside, and throwing her to the ground. Her terrified screams shattered the night. Mr. Zeitlow rushed to defend her, but he was no match for Maloney, whose brute strength proved yet again to be a terrifying tool.

Hearing the commotion, the Zeitlows' two sons raced to their parents' aid (possibly from a house nearby). But even with three men now fighting the intruder, Maloney proved to be a powerful, unrelenting opponent. The struggle dragged across the farmyard until one son, exhausted and outmatched, fell into a dire situation.

He lay helpless. Maloney was poised to strike a final blow.

But at the last dramatic moment, the other brother returned to the fight, now wielding a club. In a single decisive swing, he delivered a blow to the back of Maloney's skull.

The fight was over.

At the time, the Zeitlow family had no idea who this fallen stranger in the night was, or that he had been in custody.

Word of this wild encounter spread in sensational newspaper headlines, filled with rushed and conflicting details. Regardless, many in the region became acutely aware of a now-infamous farmer from Morrison named "Maloney the Madman."

Notably, there was public sympathy in the community for not just the Zeitlows, who were thrust into an awful situation filled with unfortunate violence, but also a great deal of compassion and remorse for Maloney, whose struggles internally led to a tragic outcome.

With all his resistance and suffering now ended, Maloney's body traveled that Sunday one last time to its final resting place. No flags were flown at half-mast—as they were for the heralded Thomas Burke discussed in the previous section—but a dignified day of mourning occurred just the same.

Maloney's burial was held in Morrison, where a large concourse of friends and relatives followed him to his gravesite.

The Founder & Electric Soap

"My wife has used Dobbins' Electric Soap and finds it excellent for taking out paint stains in clothes. She says that it promises to do wonders— but does all it promises."

These thoughts, printed in a local 1880 newspaper advertisement, represent the only lasting recorded words attributed to Alphonse Morrison, the founder of Morrison, Wisconsin.

For a man who established a town, preached sermons in the area, educated children in numerous schools, and shaped the early civic life of Brown County, it's hard to fathom that the only message that remains from this well-spoken and influential man is a trivial testimonial about soap, sandwiched between ads for dry goods and lumber.

And, for the record, Dobbins' Electric Soap had absolutely nothing to do with electricity. It was a general-purpose soap, used for hand washing, bathing, and laundry, manufactured in Philadelphia. The word "electric" was beginning to come to public attention at the time and carried the sense of something new and exciting, so an alert manufacturer appropriated the word.

As for Alphonse John Morrison, he was born in Ohio on March 5, 1817, and trained as a Methodist preacher. When he stepped into pulpits to deliver sermons, his messages about God washing away sins carried far more weight than any boasts about soap washing away paint stains.

His wife, Harriet, a devout Quaker, was also from Ohio. Her home is said to have played a role in the Underground Railroad, providing refuge for escaped slaves on their journey to Canada.

In 1847, Alphonse (often referred to as A.J.) and Harriet embarked on a westward journey by prairie schooner, navigating the dense wilderness to reach what would later become Brown County, Wisconsin. The trek was difficult, with no railroads beyond Buffalo, New York, and major cities like Chicago still little more than small towns. Alongside them on their journey were three young children, all under the age of six: sons, Salathiel and Melville, and their daughter, Celestia.

For anyone who has taken a long road trip with their children, one can only imagine how eventful this trek must have been.

Harriet was also pregnant, further adding to the difficulties.

On Feb. 8, 1851, Alphonse arrived in what would later be named the Town of Morrison, becoming the area's first settler. Surrounded by vast stretches of forest, life in this untamed land was filled with struggle. As they built their cabin, Alphonse's family lived in the very covered wagon that had carried them on their long journey.

On April 17, 1851, about ten weeks after arriving in the area, Alphonse and Harriet welcomed their second daughter into the world. This baby was the first-ever white child born in Morrison. The little girl's name was Ellen Orlena Morrison.

In 1854, the Brown County Board of Supervisors voted to officially split off a new town from the existing towns of De Pere and Wrightstown. With this new town formally created, it was suggested to name it "Morrison" in honor of Alphonse Morrison and his settlement of the area.

From there, Alphonse's log cabin became a busy and vital hub, even hosting the first-ever election of town officers.

However, the Morrison family didn't stay long in this new community that bore their name. Four years after arriving, and just one year after the town officially became his namesake, Alphonse decided to move on.

Why he left so soon is up for debate in local lore. Some dismiss his departure as a natural part of pioneer life, where individuals migrated steadily until they found the community that best suited their profession and household.

But, as is often the case in small towns, rumors have also been whispered over the years that Morrison's founder departed due to a family scandal.

It's impossible to say.

Regardless of the reason, in 1855, Alphonse sold his property in Morrison (sometimes called Morrisontown in its earliest years) and moved to nearby Wrightstown, which was named after Hoel S. Wright.

In leaving Morrison, Alphonse sold his 200-acre property to a German immigrant named Phillip Falck, who also arrived in Wisconsin under extraordinary circumstances. In 1837, at just nineteen, Falck had walked nearly 900 miles from Albany, New York, to Milwaukee, selling goods along the way to survive. That journey set the tone for a life defined by hard work and ingenuity. After marrying Catherine Hagen in 1847, the couple ventured into the wilderness of Morrison, drawn by the promise of opportunity. With the purchase of land from Morrison's founder, Falck became one of the town's first permanent anchors—and arguably its most influential pioneer.

Falck converted part of his home into Morrison's first general store, a lifeline for settlers in need of tools, dry goods, and supplies. Alongside it, he opened a tavern, and eventually a hotel,

14

creating a hub for the growing community that locals affectionately dubbed "Falck's Corner."

Over time, Falck's businesses became staples of life in Morrison, serving the lumber, farming, and cheese industries that shaped the town's economy. He even took on the role of Morrison's first postmaster and played a vital part in its spiritual life as a founding member of Morrison Zion Evangelical Lutheran Church. Through his tireless efforts, Falck and his growing family ensured the township had not just the essentials to survive, but the resources to thrive. Phillip and Catherine had ten children, many of whom also went on to become influential figures in the community.

When Phillip Falck died in 1889 at age 71, he was remembered for his kindness and charity, and how integral he was in helping town settlers overcome the many challenges of pioneer life. At his funeral, nearly 300 horse-drawn teams formed a solemn, two-mile procession—so long that people said it was the largest funeral Brown County had ever seen.

Meanwhile, Alphonse Morrison played his own integral role in Wrightstown, rather than the community that bore his name. There, he built a new wood-frame home with a brick veneer, close to the Lutheran church. He served as a teacher, postmaster, and even a mail carrier on the Star Route. His route, which spanned from Wrightstown to Cato in Manitowoc County, paid $1,000 annually—a respectable sum for the time. The position required him to deliver mail on horseback, often navigating harsh Wisconsin winters and primitive roads.

His dedication to this and other roles in Wrightstown earned him widespread respect. For example, within the soap advertisement we mentioned earlier, a note described Alphonse as one of the "best people" in the area. Some even affectionately referred to Alphonse and his wife Harriet as Grandpa and

Grandma Morrison due to the longstanding care and friendship they offered to other settlers.

Sadly, in the backdrop of this admiration (and good-natured soap testimonial), there was nothing that could remove the growing stain of heartache and tragedy that befell Alphonse's family. While the Falck family thrived and became an institution in the area, the Morrison family faced ongoing hardship. Alphonse's two sons, Salathiel and Melville, both served in the Civil War. Both enlisted in the 14th Wisconsin Infantry. Melville was just 16 years old at the time.

Salathiel, Alphonse's oldest son, was severely wounded at the Battle of Shiloh in 1862. While recovering on a hospital steamboat, he succumbed to disease—a fate that claimed more soldiers than battlefield injuries.

The family's losses continued in 1873, when both of Alphonse's daughters, Ellen and Celestia, passed away just weeks apart. Ellen, as mentioned earlier, was the first-ever child born to Town of Morrison settlers. She died at just 21 years old.

Both Morrison sisters are buried in Wrightstown.

Melville, the last surviving Morrison child, lived long enough to build a life after the war. He settled in Black Creek, where he owned a general store and played baseball, a sport growing in popularity at the time. But in 1876, tragedy struck again.

After playing baseball on an otherwise ordinary June day, he returned to his store with friends. Several of them began a game of jumping off the store steps while holding weights. After three jumps, Melville went into his store, sat on a box and began telling a war story, then fell over dead of an apparent heart attack.

In the end, all four of Alphonse and Harriet's children died before the age of 30, a stark reminder of the fragility of pioneer life.

Despite these personal hardships, Alphonse remained active in his faith, occasionally preaching sermons and filling pulpits in surrounding towns. Alphonse was also deeply involved in Sunday school work, serving as a superintendent for many years. This influence extended far beyond his immediate community, as he inspired younger generations to carry forward his values of hard work and service.

Unfortunately for Alphonse, some of his hard work and service never paid off.

Despite his efficient and personable service for nine years as postmaster in Wrightstown, which earned him widespread admiration, his tenure ended when President Grover Cleveland removed him from his position—a political decision that deeply disheartened Alphonse. Following this disappointment, he moved from the area.

His wife Harriet died in June 1893 at the age of 71 and is buried in Omro, Wisconsin.

Outliving every family member who had once huddled with him in a covered wagon during the Town of Morrison's dawning days, Alphonse eventually moved to Oklahoma. There, he spent his final years in the care of one of his granddaughters.

While he had enjoyed good health for most of his life, Alphonse's final weeks were plagued with issues… but he saw no need to address them.

He was ready for a new frontier.

As his health started to deteriorate, friends and family urged him to see a doctor, but he told them it was no use. Instead, he "talked freely of his approaching end as though he was getting ready to start on a journey."

Alphonse passed away on January 26, 1911, at the age of 94, closing the final chapter of a remarkable life. On that fateful

Thursday, he arose, dressed himself, and later lay down to rest—and passed away in his sleep.

His obituary described him as "one of nature's noblemen," paying tribute to a man known for his integrity, faith, and service to others. His body was laid to rest in Weatherford Cemetery in Oklahoma, more than 800 miles away from the town that shared his name.

There were no long funeral processions or tributes like those for Phillip Falck. Instead, "Grandpa Morrison" was laid to rest after a modest funeral held in his granddaughter's home.

Which seems rather fitting.

After all, throughout his life, Alphonse Morrison quietly fulfilled every role entrusted to him. He promised his young family a new start—and delivered it in the Wisconsin wilderness. He served his community as a teacher, preacher, and mail carrier, meeting each task with steady commitment. Whether founding a town, delivering letters through snowstorms, or standing in a pulpit, Alphonse lived a life of promises kept.

Perhaps it's also fitting, then, that the only words of his that endure—an old soap advertisement, of all things—capture the essence of his spirit: one that simply and steadily… *"does all it promises."*

A Land Before Morrison

When Joel Klug, a Morrison native, stepped into the national spotlight in 2000 as a cast member on the first season of *Survivor*, it gave him a taste of stardom at just 28 years old. The groundbreaking reality television show became a cultural phenomenon almost overnight, shattering ratings records while catapulting Klug into the public eye. For a short time, he was a household name, making guest appearances on shows like *Baywatch, Nash Bridges, The Tonight Show with Jay Leno,* and *The Late Show with David Letterman.* Magazine covers and interviews followed, marking his brief but significant brush with fame.

More than that, *Survivor* gave Klug a unique life experience. It transported him to a remote, uninhabited island in the South China Sea. This setting offered him a rare glimpse into a world untouched by human development. Having grown up in Morrison, Klug was no stranger to nature, with its woodlands and snow-covered fields, but nothing could have prepared him for the untamed, primeval landscape that greeted him on that island.

"When we hit the beach, I didn't really know what to expect. I didn't know how fake or staged it would be," Klug said years later in a local news interview. "But there was nothing. Absolutely nothing. This island they picked hadn't had people on it for 75 years. It was just a wild island. When we hit that thing, the sun was going down in a couple hours, and it just hit me: this is the real deal."

Klug lay awake that first night, hearing the harrowing sounds of wildlife scurrying about, hidden behind a blanket of trees and darkness. It was an echo of a different world, a different time.

And while he ultimately didn't win the million-dollar prize during his stint on this reality TV show, in some ways, Klug experienced a unique parallel to the harsh *reality* of Morrison's earliest settlers.

Of course, while Klug arrived on his island with cameras rolling, no technology existed in the 1800s to capture what Alphonse Morrison and his family (discussed in our previous section) encountered when they first pulled up to an untamed Wisconsin forest. There's no way to travel back in time to see firsthand what everything looked like before their arrival either.

Thankfully, we can make informed assumptions based on the accounts of early pioneers. Among the early town settlers who left us our best clues were Susan Altmeyer and Marie Rice.

Much of early Morrison's history focuses on its male settlers—farmers, soldiers, and community leaders—but the stories of Susan and Marie reveal a rare and remarkable glimpse into the realities of pioneer life through the eyes of two strong, resilient women. The journals they kept, and interviews done later in life, tell of the many dangers lurking in the woods of Morrison's earliest days.

Marie Rice came to America from Ireland in the 1850s and settled with her husband, John, in Wrightstown before moving to Morrison. Their life, like that of so many pioneers, was shaped by resilience and resourcefulness. Wolves prowled the edges of their property, and to keep them at bay, Marie placed candles in every window of her home at night. The flickering lights offered a small but vital defense against the predators that roamed the forests.

Faith was central to Marie's life and the lives of many early settlers. Before a Catholic priest regularly served Morrison, she and her neighbors walked twelve miles through the woods to attend church in De Pere. These treks began at midnight, following blazed trails through dense forests alive with the sounds of wildlife. It was a journey of both faith and survival, and each step was a testament to their determination to build a community grounded in their beliefs.

Susan Altmeyer, born in Germany in 1838, settled in Morrison with her husband before eventually moving to De Pere in 1883. During her husband's service in the Civil War, Susan managed their farm and mill alone, raising three small children in a log cabin deep in the woods. Indigenous people living in the area often came to her home, trading goods for food like flour and bacon. Susan's kindness and generosity toward them earned her the nickname "the white angel," and while these interactions with the Indigenous people were peaceful, the wilderness around her was anything but.

Like Marie Rice, Susan knew wolves were a constant threat in early Morrison. Susan regularly walked roughly 35 miles through wooded trails to Manitowoc to catch boat rides to Milwaukee. In those early days, few roads were established, so she trekked on paths that Indigenous people had carved over decades through the woods. On one of these journeys, Susan was chased by a pack of wolves and narrowly escaped with her life.

Such encounters were a harsh reminder of the dangers settlers faced daily.

The experiences of these pioneer women also highlight the struggles and ingenuity required to outwit and outlast the elements of Morrison's wilderness.

After all, there were no million-dollar prizes in the real-life drama of their era. The stakes were real. The threats were constant. And sometimes, people simply didn't *survive*.

In 1859, the bodies of an Indigenous hunter in Morrison and a massive bear were discovered in the woods. The hunter had mortally wounded the bear, but in its final moments, the animal attacked and killed him. In the end, this mighty beast and brave man lay dead together in the thick forest, the air from their lungs stolen for eternity. This tragic encounter provides another dramatic glimpse into the dangers of the untamed land.

Bears remained a looming threat in the community for decades. In September 1894, a bear living by a swamp between Morrison and Cooperstown raided local farms at night, carrying off sheep and calves.

Needless to say, the town's sprawling woods could be a frightening place.

It's no wonder that panic spread in Morrison in 1871 when a child wandered off and got lost in the woods… for *days*. The youngster was only around three years old at the time and disappeared on a Friday. Morrison residents poured into the forest to search for the missing toddler, and thankfully found the child on the following Monday, still alive but weak from not eating.

Over the course of four summer days and three harrowing nights, the lost youngster wandered nearly two miles from where they first entered the woods. The fact that the child only needed a meal, and had not become one, was arguably a miracle.

But, of course, beyond risk and danger, there was also beauty in nature—and the land before Morrison flourished with it.

Herds of deer enjoyed the vast canopy of trees to protect them in harsh winters. Speckled trout thrived in the Branch River. Scores of birds fluttered above. A variety of wildlife spread to all corners of the region.

And they weren't alone.

Indigenous peoples, like those that visited Susan Altmeyer or fell victim to a mighty bear, thrived in the area for centuries. Before our roads, homes, churches, and any "white angels" came along, these people created generations of their own memories and traditions within the woods.

In fact, one young girl growing up in Morrison during the pioneer era later recalled playing on a sandpile near her family's farmstead when an Indigenous woman came walking down the road. The woman was carrying a child on her back, waving a cloth as she shouted. The little girl remembered watching this from a distance, torn between curiosity and fear, intrigued by a way of life that stretched back long before her own.

But everything changed for them. This was, admittedly, not unique to the Town of Morrison.

Mirroring similar outcomes elsewhere in Wisconsin, forests were logged out by arriving pioneers, the land reshaped for farming, and the way of life for the Indigenous people was shattered. Forced relocations in Wisconsin sent many to reservations or scattered them far from their ancestral lands.

Animals that once dominated the region also faced their own upheavals.

Hunting provided essential food and materials for settlers. One recorded example took place in October 1887, when Peter Heimel of Morrison shot a deer weighing 211 pounds.

Other times, hunting helped rid the area of dangerous threats. This included wildcats (or bobcats), which often lurked in the region throughout the late 1800s. A few examples include one bobcat killed near Glenmore in 1897, and another large bobcat killed by a Morrison hunter in November 1899.

But, sometimes, hunting seemed to happen... simply because it could. In 1884, a man in Wayside captured a rare turkey buzzard (or vulture), an event so unusual it made local headlines due to how fast the species was dwindling in Brown County. Some settlers also kept wild animals as pets or trophies, with photographs from the era showing farmers posing proudly with foxes on chains. These small moments of control over nature eventually became much larger patterns that literally changed the area's landscape forever.

Some animals adapted to the changing environment, while others were forced to relocate. Some vanished entirely. Wolves and bears, once common sights in Morrison, saw their populations decimated as forests were cleared and hunting intensified.

Now, unlike the time of Susan Altmeyer and Marie Rice, no candles are needed to fend off predators when the sun goes down. In fact, a wolf or bear sighting in the town these days would be rather rare and remarkable, giving a special glimpse of "survivors" from a bygone era.

The Union Hotel, Social Security, & the Green Bay Packers

When Nicholas and Susan Altmeyer put down roots in the fledgling town of Morrison, they could never have imagined the lasting impact their family would have—not only on the region but on national institutions like American government and professional sports.

And, yes, this is the same Susan we mentioned in our previous section. Also, note… the surname Altmeyer shifted at some point to the spelling Altmayer, so it may appear differently at times throughout this chapter.

The Altmeyers joined Morrison's first residents around 1860, about a half decade after the town's founding. There, they began building a life together, working on their farm and operating a sawmill.

When Nicholas was called away to serve in the Civil War, Susan was left to manage both the farm and their three young children alone (they later had nine total). Despite these challenges, Susan endured and also embraced innovation. She purchased one of the first sewing machines in the county for $150—a near fortune at the time. Neighboring women brought fabric to her home to have clothing made on the machine while Susan juggled farmwork and childcare.

After Nicholas returned from the war, he resumed his role in the community, serving as a town supervisor and treasurer. His efforts helped shape the town's early identity and strengthen its foundation.

However, in 1873, disaster struck: their family's sawmill burned to the ground, causing an $8,000 uninsured loss. Despite the setback, the Altmeyers persisted for another decade in Morrison, but by 1883, they were ready for a change.

After all, life in a young and rugged settlement often required the courage to adapt and take risks. In this case, it meant leaving the familiarity of Morrison, a place they had spent nearly a quarter century, and uprooting the family for a new adventure.

After selling their farm, the family wasn't sure where they would head to next but eventually embarked on a new project in De Pere—a community about a dozen miles from Morrison. The project? A hotel and tavern named the Union House, a tribute to the Union Army that Nicholas had served during the war. The Union House, later known as the Union Hotel, quickly became an area institution.

Situated on the corner of Broadway and James Street, the Union Hotel charged guests $1 a night—a modest rate that made it popular with travelers. With business booming, Nicholas expanded the hotel within its first year.

However, success in this new city eventually came at the cost of family turmoil. By the summer of 1899, about a decade and a half after building the Union Hotel, Nicholas's behavior and whereabouts became murky, at best. Soon after selling the Union Hotel to his son, Fred, Nicholas went missing for several weeks. Rumors spread that he was involved with a local divorced woman, with sightings of him and the woman checking into a hotel in

Ashland. The scandal stained his reputation in De Pere, where Nicholas had been a deputy sheriff, a member of the fire department, and an ex-alderperson. Though Nicholas returned to clear the air, insisting he had been away on business, the damage to his name was clear.

His status as a deputy sheriff in De Pere was quickly revoked.

When ownership of the Union Hotel eventually passed from the Altmeyers to the Maternoski family, it steadily grew in renown—later forging a connection with another Wisconsin icon: the Green Bay Packers.

For roughly 40 years, the Union Hotel was the long-term home of tenant Gerald "Dad" Braisher. Braisher rented an upstairs room and worked as the Packers' equipment manager from 1956 to 1977. He came to the Packers after a 33-year career as an industrial arts teacher and championship-winning sports coach in De Pere.

In 1961, the story goes that a far more legendary coach—Vince Lombardi—asked Braisher to help design a logo for the Packers' plain helmets. Working at night in his room at the Union Hotel, Braisher sketched out a concept of the now-iconic "G" logo—not for "Green Bay," but allegedly for "Greatness."

While Braisher worked on his sketches upstairs in the Union Hotel, he occasionally brought rough drafts down to the bar to get feedback. A St. Norbert College art student later helped refine the design, which Lombardi approved. Today, the logo Braisher helped create remains one of the most recognized symbols in professional sports.

While the Altmayers' old hotel was a backdrop for creating "green and gold" icons on the football field, a family member was busy helping with green and gold in a different way in Washington.

The Altmayer's grandson, Arthur J. Altmeyer, played a pivotal role in creating America's Social Security system—a far more notable role in politics than his grandfather's tenure as the Town of Morrison supervisor decades earlier. As Chairman of the Federal Social Security Administration, Arthur's legacy reached into the lives of millions.

In 1953, after President Dwight D. Eisenhower took office, the position of Commissioner for Social Security was eliminated, replaced by a newly structured office. The change effectively ended Arthur Altmeyer's career just days before he would have qualified for full retirement benefits. In response to public outcry, the Eisenhower administration offered him a one-month appointment so he could retire with benefits—but Altmeyer refused, unwilling to accept pay for what he viewed as a meaningless title.

Arthur Altmeyer passed away in 1972. After his death, the Social Security Administration honored his legacy by naming its Baltimore headquarters' Administration Building after him.

He wasn't the only Altmeyer grandchild to have a building named after them.

Susie Altmayer, granddaughter of Nicholas and Susan, became a beloved teacher and principal in De Pere. In her honor, Susie C. Altmayer Elementary School was opened and named after her in 2007, a tribute to her lasting contributions to local education and community life.

Susie C. Altmayer Elementary School is situated roughly three miles from the Union Hotel.

At the time of this book's publication, the Union Hotel, still operated by the Maternoski/Boyd family for multiple generations, continues as a fine-dining institution in De Pere.

And as for that green and gold football team with its iconic "G" logo, the Union Hotel has been visited by many of its Hall of Fame players—and virtually every Packers coach in the team's history, including champions like Curly Lambeau in the 1920s and

Vince Lombardi in the 1960s. Lombardi stopped visiting, however, after bringing friends from New York one night for a late dinner. The group was not served their meal due to ordering it after the kitchen closed. Rules were rules at the Union Hotel, regardless of customer notoriety. That didn't stop other legends (and champions) from coming. Coach Mike Holmgren celebrated the Packers' victory over the Carolina Panthers in the 1996 NFC Championship Game by heading to the Union Hotel with friends.

He went on to win the Super Bowl two weeks later.

With this victory, Holmgren's Packers became Green Bay legends, remembered for their toughness, their triumphs, and their Lambeau Leaps. But well before that era, the Altmeyers took a different leap—one less visible, but every bit as defining.

When Nicholas and Susan sold their farm in Morrison, they didn't know where that gamble would lead. But their fresh start in De Pere set into motion a legacy far larger than a burned sawmill or a small farm could have offered. From a respected and iconic restaurant to vital national policy, from local education to building the birthplace of one of sports' most recognizable logos, the Altmeyers' story began with leaving Morrison after more than 20 years of memories… and then leaving a mark far, far beyond it.

Wayside's Sore Winners

If you've walked the halls of Morrison and Wayside schools in modern times, you're bound to see the glistening reflection of sports trophies, many won through the hard work, skill, and noble sportsmanship of student-athletes.

Adults also have a rich history of sport in the town, forming or partaking in various baseball, softball, football, volleyball, and basketball leagues, or seeking glory on local bowling lanes or nearby golf courses over the years.

But where did it all start?

We'll never know for sure, but the first known mention of sports in town came during a Fourth of July bash in 1879, when Morrison's residents gathered for a day of celebration, dancing, and fun. During the festivities, a baseball game and a foot race were organized. Sizable cash prizes awaited the triumphant souls who won these contests.

Of course, as time went on, not every race ended with prizes and proud winners.

Take, for example, Grey Prince, Morrison's first recorded "loser" in competition—not a person, but a horse. In 1890, Grey Prince carried Morrison's hopes in a race at the De Pere Driving Park (now known as the Brown County Fairgrounds). At the event, Grey Prince faced off against two fierce opponents: Fanny Fern and Bay Billy.

The race didn't go well for Morrison's steed.

While Fanny Fern took the crown and Bay Billy claimed second place, Morrison's Grey Prince seemed completely out of his league. As newspapers of the time delicately put it, Grey Prince was "not in it at any time."

Still, let's give credit where credit is due: Grey Prince may have been slow, but he finished the race. That's more than we can say for some of Morrison's human competitors, whose antics are perhaps even more disappointing.

Remember the old adage that "winners never quit, and quitters never win"? Well, during one strange year in pioneer history, a team from Wayside seemed determined to challenge that saying— repeatedly.

The saga started in the winter months of early 1908, when men from Wayside represented Morrison in a basketball contest at nearby Cato. The battle on the hardwood ended with neither team winning, thanks to a peculiar set of circumstances involving the visiting team.

Accounts of this unusual basketball game differ slightly, but the score was around 25 points apiece late in the battle, with Wayside clinging to a narrow lead. Throughout the contest, Cato suffered large deficits and was said to be a much smaller squad compared to the "giants" from Wayside. But they had grit and determination. Victory even seemed within reach for the small hometown heroes, against all odds.

But then, in a strange twist… confusion, or perhaps *collusion*, struck. With a mere four and a half minutes remaining, the game was abruptly called off by a Wayside timekeeper.

It is said that Wayside "got cold feet" and decided to quit.

Sort of.

Apparently, Wayside's own "professional referee" refused to declare the game forfeited. According to one loyal Cato supporter, after the official told the Wayside team privately that he believed they would lose if they played the game out, rather than risk defeat, Wayside walked off the court instead.

Perhaps not noble, but it was certainly a creative way to avoid losing.

But if you think these antics on the basketball court reek of being sore losers and quitters, hang tight! That same year, Wayside proved they could also be sore winners.

In the autumn of 1908, the men of Wayside swapped their basketballs for baseball gloves. This time, their sporting escapades led them to Kellnersville, where they took to the baseball diamond for what should have been a friendly game. Unfortunately, the contest devolved into a circus of poor officiating and mounting frustrations.

Kellnersville found themselves battling not only the Wayside team, but also a visiting umpire whose judgment could generously be described as "questionable." The home team was outraged by the umpire's one-sided calls. If news reports are to be believed, fair hits were deemed foul, and the already difficult task of scoring became a daunting challenge.

For one team, that is.

The umpire, a Wayside man, wasn't subtle about his bias. Allegedly, whenever Kellnersville posed a scoring threat, the umpire's vision seemed to fail him. A report from Manitowoc claimed that "it usually took *six* balls to draw a pass on which to reach first base, while with men on the sacks, *one* strike was sufficient to retire the locals."

For Kellnersville, this felt less like a baseball game and more like an elaborate farce. Their frustration boiled over, and by the sixth inning, the locals had seen enough. Kellnersville forfeited the game, declaring that it was impossible to win against both an opposing team and an umpire.

The incident was called the "worst deal ever" given to Kellnersville's sluggers. One newspaper even remarked, "It grieves us to think that the visitors possess no more manly instincts than they exhibited here." Wayside left town with what was described as a "dishonorable victory and a lemon."

And so, for at least one strange year, Wayside's pioneer athletes cemented a place in local sporting lore, not through grit or glory, but by proving that even if "quitters never win," they can keep dodging losses—especially if they bring an ally in stripes.

Quarrels Over Quarantine

An "anti-vaxxer" in Morrison's pioneer days? Outrage over quarantines? We'll get to that in a moment.

But first, let's start with something we might relate to more closely. Depending on your age, you (or an older relative of yours) probably remember the health saga of 2020—COVID-19. During this era, discussions of vaccines and quarantines burned red-hot across the globe. It was a time of frightening possibilities, uncertainty, and emotional turmoil. Most who lived through it still have strong opinions about it to this day.

As spring 2020 arrived, global health officials scrambled to understand the new coronavirus's gravity. Hospitals became overwhelmed. Stores, schools, and offices closed or adapted to virtual formats. Social distancing became routine, as did masks after Wisconsin Governor Tony Evers issued a mandate in August 2020. In Morrison, hand sanitizer stations popped up in schools and churches, and people adjusted to new norms.

COVID-19 symptoms ranged from mild to catastrophic, leaving some families blindsided and grieving and others scratching their heads wondering why any precautions were happening at all. Debates over regulations, mask mandates, and— most volatile of all—vaccines dominated public discourse. The

34

first vaccines in late 2020 were welcomed by some and viewed with suspicion by others.

Those who rejected them declared themselves "anti-vaxxers," while supporters praised science.

Alas, people have always been complicated—and public health has always been complicated, too.

As history shows us, what happened with COVID-19 was far from unprecedented. Morrison itself faced eerily similar debates and controversies in the pioneer era. In fact, the 1880s saw similar clashes over vaccines, quarantine, and public health.

Long before anyone had heard of COVID-19, smallpox was one of the deadliest threats to communities like Morrison. Smallpox, a disfiguring, contagious, and often fatal illness, haunted early settlers. With a 30% fatality rate, survivors often bore deep scars and permanent disfigurement. Quarantine, inoculation, and vaccines were used to combat diseases, but it didn't erase resistance.

In February 1882, Morrison experienced a smallpox outbreak linked to Miss Schunk, a resident who caught the disease in nearby De Pere. She returned home instead of quarantining.

Horrified, locals condemned this decision, labeling it "reprehensible."

Smallpox spreads through droplets and remains contagious until scabs fall off. Tragically, Miss Schunk died, and two more family members succumbed soon after. The entire household fell ill, fueling further fears and outrage over the lack of precautions—a sentiment that echoes the controversies of future pandemics.

Smallpox wasn't the only frightening illness Morrison faced in this era. Diphtheria also left a painful mark on the community, claiming at least seventeen young lives and, in several cases, taking more than one child from the same family. Often called the "strangling angel," the disease earned its grim nickname for the thick, gray membrane that could form in a victim's throat. Once it appeared, the "strangling" would begin. Breathing became increasingly difficult until the airway closed completely, leading to suffocation. For pioneer parents, losing children to this horrible fate was a terrifying and real possibility. But over time, medical advances—including vaccinations—helped bring the disease under control.

Even so, pioneer diseases like diphtheria and smallpox unfolded during a cultural crossroads, when debates over contagion, quarantine, and vaccination were growing louder across Wisconsin. Against the backdrop of these rising debates, Morrison found itself linked to a bizarre public health episode, courtesy of one of Wisconsin's most infamous "anti-vaxxers," Dr. Matthew Rodermund.

Dr. Rodermund, an Appleton physician, initially adhered to accepted scientific norms. But by 1900, he declared that smallpox, diphtheria, and other illnesses were not contagious. He also dismissed vaccines and quarantines as scams. To "prove" his point, Dr. Rodermund staged dramatic demonstrations. He once rubbed smallpox pus into his hands, face, and clothing, then mingled with patients, friends, and the public.

Appleton residents were understandably horrified. His actions made headlines, and the backlash was swift. His children were barred from schools, his son expelled from college, and the local men's club revoked his membership. The family was socially shunned.

Unfazed, Rodermund reportedly declared, "If they quarantine me, it will only be over my dead body."

Authorities obliged. Armed police officers quarantined him and his family in their Appleton home. But the ever-dramatic Rodermund wasn't done. He somehow escaped confinement—possibly with help—leading to a media frenzy. Newspapers printed diagrams of his escape route. He fled to Chicago, then Milwaukee, where he was arrested.

Despite fines, lawsuits, and threats to revoke his medical license, Dr. Rodermund continued his anti-vaccine crusade. He also promoted other unconventional medical theories, including his claim that appendicitis should not be treated with surgery. In 1918, he was charged in Madison for performing an illegal operation on a woman.

His antics left a lasting impression, and his influence intertwined with the Town of Morrison. Years earlier, Morrison had its own state-appointed Health Officer, Dr. Edward Booth Kendall, who initially championed vaccination and reported disease outbreaks. In 1894, he vaccinated 300 schoolchildren, lamenting when others refused. But after moving to Menasha, he fell under Dr. Rodermund's influence.

Dr. Kendall's beliefs shifted dramatically as a result. In the early 1900s, he stopped reporting smallpox cases, ignored quarantines, and faced legal charges for neglecting public health duties. Menasha residents claimed that Kendall instructed local families to keep quiet if their children showed any symptoms of smallpox or diphtheria, even allowing them to visit relatives rather than quarantine.

Rodermund defended Kendall during his trial, but Kendall was convicted and fined. Like his mentor, the former Morrison health officer retained his license despite his actions.

Together, Kendall and Rodermund co-wrote articles promoting their ideas. While their influence faded over time, their story—and the parallels between Morrison's smallpox era and the COVID-19 pandemic—highlight how enduring tensions exist around health, science, and who decides what counts as information or misinformation.

As history shows, smallpox was eventually eradicated in 1980 through a public-health campaign that included widespread vaccination. Yet for COVID-19 and other modern diseases, debates over their causes, treatments, and prevention persist.

So, it seems that no matter how much science advances, human nature will remain constant.

And with that, perhaps there's only one thing we can all agree on: In every era, we'll need to battle not only the problems of our times, but also the strong opinions that come with them.

Dark & Stormy Nights

There's an old saying: "When thunder roars, go indoors." But fate doesn't always grant that option. On June 10, 1880, 17-year-old Julia Pepper became an unfortunate storm casualty when lightning struck her as she worked in her father's wheat field in Morrison.

Her death was the beginning of a tragic pattern in Morrison's early history.

Lightning strikes are rare—affecting less than one in a million people—but when they happen, the force is beyond the stuff of nightmares. A single strike delivers millions of volts, with temperatures hotter than the surface of the sun.

Even indoor environments aren't always safe.

In homes without proper grounding, lightning can travel through walls, floors, and pipes, leading to injuries, fires, and fatalities. This wasn't uncommon in the pioneer years.

Benjamin Franklin's invention of the lightning rod in 1756 provided a measure of protection, but rural adoption lagged behind. Some farmers were reluctant to invest in the unfamiliar technology, leaving homes and barns vulnerable. Scams didn't help either, with a Morrison farmer getting swindled out of $250 in 1899 by "lightning rod sharpers."

Three years after Julia's death, lightning struck again in Morrison, this time in the home of Herman Trapp, shattering the chimney and ripping through the roof and floors. The bolt stopped just below the bed of Trapp's 9-month-old daughter, who survived with a leg injury caused by flying wood. Strangely, some speculated that the injury might help heal her already-diseased leg. Whether it did is unknown, but the story stands as one of Morrison's odd tales of survival.

Just weeks later, on July 24, 1883, a storm described as "the most fearful of wind and rain" in the region's history struck Morrison again. The sky darkened "almost as intense as midnight," and fifteen minutes of violent winds demolished buildings, homes, and barns. The wind was so fierce that fences were swept away, roofs on several barns flew off, stretches of forest were torn apart, and orchards were destroyed, with some trees flattened and the fruit stripped from those that remained. The downpour of rain was so dense that it was almost impossible to see anything. During the storm, lightning killed two cows each belonging to J.C. Brill and James Sullivan, and several barns were struck. Though damage was widespread, no human lives are known to have been lost.

But, the following year, lightning returned with tragic consequences.

At the home of Jason Schunk, lightning traveled down the chimney, through the stove, and across the floor. One of Schunk's sons was thrown backward over ten yards but emerged unharmed. His brother, Daniel, sitting in a chair, wasn't as fortunate. The current passed through him, killing him instantly.

In just five years, two young lives—Julia Pepper and Daniel Schunk—were taken by lightning's rare and devastating force.

Horses were sometimes the unlucky victims of storms as well. In July 1879, an unusual tragedy struck the Morrison area when lightning penetrated the stable of Carl Treichel, killing his pair of horses. Strangely, there was no visible damage to either the building or the animals. The very same event occurred across the road at the Riley farm, where one of their horses was also found dead in its stall. The owners believed both sets of animals were killed by the same bolt. Treichel received $70 in insurance compensation, but the Rileys had allowed their policy to lapse just before the freak accident.

Other financial losses mounted from storms in Morrison's pioneer era. For example, lightning struck August Haese's sawmill in October 1920, destroying valuable lumber and causing thousands of dollars in uninsured damage. Eight years later, in 1928, lightning hit Emma Schelter's property, destroying her barn, garage, and outbuildings, with losses totaling $10,000—roughly $174,000 today.

The most destructive storms often paired lightning with high winds and tornado-like conditions. In 1870, a severe storm hit Morrison and caused extensive damage. At least one roof was blown off a house, and the fierce winds scattered other smaller items around the town. In 1887, the roof of Charles Natzke's home came flying off in a storm.

In May 1930, hail piled four inches high against buildings, and cyclonic winds tore apart structures. In Wayside, a chicken brooder was flung against a house, igniting a fire that killed 100 chicks. Across Morrison, barns, silos, and windmills collapsed, scattering debris over fields.

These storms resembled tornadoes, though the term was rarely used at the time. Before the mid-20th century, weather services avoided the word "tornado" to prevent panic. It wasn't until the 1960s, with advances in forecasting and warning systems, that tornado preparation became more systematic. Until then, some storms struck without warning, leaving communities to pick up the pieces.

In more modern times, a strong windstorm in the summer of 2013 also wreaked havoc unexpectedly, toppling trees, damaging homes, and destroying barns throughout the community—giving residents a small taste of what early settlers once faced in their own fierce battles with Mother Nature.

War

War creates death and suffering on an unparalleled scale: gunfire, explosions, shattered bones, and minds left scarred. Survivors often carry the trauma of the battlefield long after the sounds of war have faded. For the people of Morrison, the Civil War was the first of many conflicts to leave its mark, reshaping the town and its residents in profound ways.

It was also the backdrop of a highly unusual journey for one local man.

Most soldiers in the Civil War naturally joined one side—but not Timothy Reidy, an Irish immigrant from Morrison whose wartime journey defied expectations. Born in 1833, Reidy came to Morrison in 1854, where he built a cabin and carved out a life on the frontier. By 1861, however, he found himself in an unlikely place—Texas.

How exactly Reidy ended up in the South at the outbreak of war is uncertain, but what is known is he enlisted in Cook's Heavy Artillery, a Confederate unit. Local newspaper accounts later said that "against his will [Reidy] was forced to fight on the side of the South" and that his military service "was almost that of constant battle and warfare during a period of four years." This included the Battle of Sabine Pass, one of the South's unlikely victories. During this battle, he recognized several captured Union soldiers from his earlier days in Boston and, through them, was able to send a letter to his family in Morrison.

This was the first word they had received from him in years.

But Reidy's service under the Confederate flag would not last. By 1865, he had deserted, escaping into Mexico, being held up by bandits there for a short while, before finally making his way to Union-controlled New Orleans. There, he reenlisted—this time for the North. He was assigned to a unit transporting supplies to Fort Kearney in Wyoming, serving out the remainder of the war under the same banner as his fellow Wisconsinites.

But that time was brief.

Less than two weeks after taking up arms for the Union, and before ever having a chance to rejoin the battlefield, General Robert E. Lee surrendered.

After Reidy's military service ended, he returned to Morrison in 1866 but later moved to Missouri. In 1915, he came back to Morrison once more and remained there until his death in 1925. He was buried in a Catholic cemetery in Maple Grove.

Reidy's story is just one example of how war shaped Morrison—not just in the lives it claimed, but in the lives it forever altered.

When the Civil War first erupted in 1861, Morrison was a young town, barely six years old. It was still forging its identity in Wisconsin's untamed landscape, but like the rest of the country, it was swept up in the conflict. Families were divided as men marched off to war, many never to return.

The Civil War remains the deadliest conflict in American history, with an estimated 750,000 lives lost—more than in both World Wars combined.

Countless others were wounded, many losing limbs or suffering permanent disabilities. The war also left emotional scars as deep as the physical ones, shaping lives and communities in ways that would ripple through generations. In some heartbreaking cases, reports of traumatized veterans later dying by suicide were not unheard of.

As discussed in a previous chapter, even Morrison's founder and namesake, Alphonse Morrison, was not spared from the horrors of war. Two of his sons fought in the Civil War, with one dying during the war itself and the other passing away from an apparent heart attack before the age of 30. For a family that had already endured the hardships of pioneer life, such losses must have been nearly unbearable.

Other stories of Morrison's Civil War veterans reflect the unwavering loyalty and sacrifice of soldiers. Michael Rourke, a former Morrison resident, was fatally wounded at the Battle of Perryville in Tennessee in 1862. He suffered a shot through his left lung.

After being shot, despite his own grave injuries, Rourke's mind shifted immediately to his loved ones back home. He handed $135 to a nearby soldier, with instructions to send it to his brother. Rourke was then transported for medical care and lived for fifteen days before passing away. During his painful final weeks, he again confirmed with his captain, Thomas Green, that the money he left would be sent back to his family in Morrison.

Green ensured the man's dying wish was honored.

Rourke's loving deathbed gesture struck a chord with the captain, and he wrote a letter to the fallen soldier's family to send along with the money. In one section of the letter, he wrote "Michael was one of my best men; he was never sick and always done his duty well. He fought nobly… and never faltered until he fell mortally wounded."

While this letter unquestionably meant a lot to Rourke's family in Morrison, it couldn't change the grim reality that their lives were forever altered.

Indeed, life on the battlefield was brutal, and war's toll was just as heavy at home. The men left to fight, but the women and children of Morrison bore their own battles—keeping farms running, tending livestock, raising children and siblings, and waiting for their own letters that sometimes never came.

The physical and emotional labor required to sustain a household without its primary provider was immense. Little is recorded about the women of early Morrison, but they were the unheralded backbone of the town, holding families together while their husbands, fathers, and brothers fought.

The legacy of war in Morrison's pioneer years didn't end with the Civil War. World War I pulled more young adults from the town's farms and fields and sent them across the Atlantic to fight in Europe's trenches. At least one of them, Private Wesley Saenger, never returned. He was killed in action in France on October 5, 1918, just weeks before the war ended. He had told his widowed mother and brother, before leaving for war, that if he died, he wished to be buried on American soil.

As fate would have it, this wish had many sad and unusual twists and turns.

Saenger, a member of the 128th Infantry Regiment, left for Europe in May and quickly found himself facing brutal combat against German forces. His regiment fought with such intensity that they earned the French nickname Les Terribles.

When he was tragically killed (instantly by a piece of shrapnel), he was buried in a trench on a battlefield in France, alongside four other American victims. Saenger lay buried there for nearly seven years. Beside him was a drinking cup, eleven pieces of French money, and one Chinese coin. He was also wearing an amethyst birthstone ring.

Ironically, the ring that signified his birth eventually helped him in death. Long after the war ended, the United States Army was still trying to recover bodies lost in battle, and Saenger's ring was used to confirm his identity. The military returned the ring to his mother Anna. She also requested his body be sent home, in accordance with his wish. It took several months for her lost son to arrive, but he finally made it back in the summer of 1926.

Saenger was laid to rest in Lark beside his father in a solemn military funeral. It was an emotional event for the region, attended by roughly 2,000 people.

Given how much time had passed since "The Great War," some news outlets noted that Saenger's funeral might be "Brown County's last military funeral."

If only that were true.

World War II reignited global chaos—more death and suffering on an unparalleled scale—not even fifteen years later.

During World War II, Corporal Ambrose Stedl of Morrison was killed on August 8, 1944, while serving with the 743rd Tank Battalion—a unit that had stormed the beaches of Normandy just two months earlier. Like Saenger's family before them, Stedl's loved ones first received word that he was "missing in action." Days later, their worst fears were confirmed. He had died in combat.

These are just a few of the many war stories forged by Morrison residents. Sadly, there are far too many to mention here.

From the Civil War to modern times, Morrison's history is intertwined with military service. For more than 175 years, residents of Morrison and Brown County have answered the call, enduring the horrors of war and returning, when they could, to rebuild their lives and their community.

The tales of those who served—whether they perished on distant battlefields or returned home to tell their stories—are a reminder of the sacrifices that have shaped not only Morrison's past, but our country's, too.

That said, the very notion of our country going to war wasn't always without its share of disagreement and controversy in Morrison. We'll explore why in our next chapter.

Loyal – Or Not?

When the United States declared war on Germany on April 2, 1917, a wave of intense patriotism swept the nation, making almost anything German seem suspect. Sauerkraut became known as "Liberty Cabbage," and many people with German names, like Schmidt and Mueller, anglicized them to "Smith" and "Miller." Schools dropped German language courses, and, in extreme cases, individuals speaking German were detained as suspected spies.

At the same time, the U.S. government issued Liberty Loans—government bonds aimed at raising funds for the war effort. Marketed as a patriotic investment, these bonds allowed ordinary Americans to support the military financially and demonstrate their loyalty. In many communities, patriotism was measured by its participation in Liberty Loan drives.

Towns were expected to meet or exceed quotas.

But, in the Green Bay area, Morrison fell under scrutiny during World War I for its perceived German leanings. A significant number of Morrison residents were of German descent, and some still spoke German at home. Local churches even offered German services in addition to English ones. During the charged atmosphere of the time, Morrison's ethnic and linguistic ties became a source of deeper suspicion.

One event that fueled these suspicions was a special 1918 election for a U.S. Senate seat, where voters could choose between the major party candidates or a Socialist from Milwaukee, Victor Berger. Later indicted under the 1918 Espionage Act, Berger was seen by some as a "pro German" candidate. Morrison's tally of 177 votes for Berger became, to some, evidence of disloyalty.

Tensions intensified that April when a Green Bay newspaper ran the inflammatory headline: "Kaiser's Town of Morrison is Invaded by Loyalists." This referred to Wilhelm II, Germany's emperor (or *kaiser*). The article cited an incident involving Liberty Loan representatives visiting Morrison and described the town as "The Prussian stronghold in Brown County." The report went on to say, "Within its limits, German is the language of the majority, English of the minority; disloyalty is considered a virtue and loyalty a vice. 'Die Wacht Am Rhein' is popular, and 'The Star-Spangled Banner' is unpopular."

In the rhetoric of 1918, such pointed language implied Morrison was a nest of enemy sympathizers.

The event that sparked the accusation of disloyalty involved Liberty Loan organizer A. M. Eberhardt from Chicago, who was on a fundraising campaign in the Green Bay region. He stopped in Morrison to speak at a Lutheran church but received a cold reception.

How cold?

According to Eberhardt, "I have talked on subjects connected with the war in five middle western states. I have talked in communities notoriously noted for their pro-German population. And I have never before received as frosty and hostile a greeting as in this village."

Eberhardt was asked to wait in an unheated room until the minister, who conducted services in German, put his speaking request to a congregational vote. It took two ballots for the congregation to grant Eberhardt permission, and his speech received little enthusiasm—unlike the warm welcome he had grown accustomed to elsewhere.

Not all Morrison residents were unwelcoming. Eberhardt reported having lunch with a businessman of German descent who wore Liberty Loan and Red Cross buttons. But this businessman, with two sons serving in France, told Eberhardt that his pro-American stance had hurt his business.

Obviously, this didn't help Eberhardt's view of the community.

After stopping in Morrison, Eberhardt traveled to Wayside, where he received polite but muted applause, with no American flags or Liberty Loan posters displayed. He received a warm welcome only after reaching Greenleaf, where American flags, Liberty Loan posters, and enlistment displays adorned the hall, and the audience opened and closed the meeting with patriotic songs.

In 1918, these were all seen as hallmarks of loyalty: subscribing to the Liberty Loan, displaying flags, speaking English, and singing patriotic songs. By these standards, Morrison fell short in the eyes of some critics, especially as German Americans throughout the town continued to speak German and failed to visibly demonstrate their patriotism.

A few days after the unflattering article was printed criticizing the Morrison community, several people from the town traveled to Green Bay to defend their loyalty.

The paper claimed Morrison residents wanted a chance to prove their patriotism and "to show they have adopted a different attitude." The Lutheran congregation where Eberhardt experienced his chilly reception also published a statement asserting they had been misunderstood. The church noted it was uncommon in their congregation for anyone but the minister to stand in front of their gatherings. Speeches or political activity, they said, felt uncomfortable in their place of worship.

If that weren't enough, the church sought to eliminate any doubt in their statement by writing bluntly: "We are not Teutons, not Germans, but 'LOYAL AMERICAN CITIZENS.'"

Nevertheless, the newspaper remained skeptical, remarking that Morrison's 177 votes for Berger "was a solid, pro-German vote, giving, wittingly or unwittingly, aid and comfort to the enemy."

In May 1918, tensions further escalated when George Lemke from Morrison was fined for alleged disloyalty. Reportedly, Lemke drove Liberty Loan officers off his father's farm and refused to subscribe, also remarking he would not sell his grain to the government unless he obtained "his price."

Lemke's case at municipal court was the first of its kind in Brown County. He was fined $500.

Perhaps those selling Liberty Loans could be a bit chilly, too. Local officials believed the farmer's fine (equivalent to about $10,000 in today's money), would "serve as an example to any disloyalists who might in the future voice their sentiments in protest of the government's war program." Lemke, for his part, simply paid the fine and moved on, wanting the drama to fade away.

Still, others in the Morrison community pushed back at what they felt was an unfair characterization of their town. A letter to the editor in that same month claimed four Morrison school districts had oversubscribed to the Liberty Loan.

This was waved off by another newspaper account, attributing any support in Morrison to be coming from "Hibernians and Bohemians" living there. In fact, one angry journalist noted that two town officials hadn't contributed to the loan at all, calling for their removal.

It was becoming clear that no matter what residents of Morrison did, swaying public opinion would be difficult. But gradually, things changed. Scrutiny over Morrison's loyalty continued for a while, but the frosty view of the community eventually started to thaw. Later reports acknowledged that the town met its Liberty Loan quotas. And, after the war ended in November 1918, patriotic fervor gradually faded, too—along with the tensions and suspicions that had briefly put Morrison's loyalty in the spotlight.

In decades to follow, new wars came and went, but school picnics in the town were filled with happy adults and children, smiling, waving American flags, and singing patriotic tunes.

Drama

Frank Frosch of Wayside was an enterprising man and a prominent figure in early Morrison. He founded several businesses and made lasting contributions to the town, many of which continue to thrive today. Perhaps his most recognizable project still serving the community (as of 2025) is a tavern built in 1890. Though it's had various owners and names over the years, modern visitors know it as Sally B's Tavern or DeGreef's, a popular rural pub in Wayside.

Regardless of its name, like many small-town Wisconsin taverns, it has long served as a spot to enjoy food, drinks, and spirited debates with friends, neighbors, and even strangers.

Before constructing what would become this long-serving bar, Frosch was busy building other local staples, including a large store, a successful dance hall, a cheese factory, and a windmill that supplied water to his home and factory.

At the time, the windmill was hardly remarkable—just another piece of rural infrastructure. Windmills were essential in the late 1800s and early 1900s, providing water and powering mills. They were beautiful, practical tools that helped ease the burden of manual labor for settlers. Morrison was no exception.

Another windmill, built in 1904 by August Griepentrog, Morrison's town clerk for over 20 years, was similarly unremarkable but welcome. Newspaper reports labeled it "a great enhancement" to Griepentrog's property, which highlights how common and appreciated these structures were.

For something so ordinary in early Morrison, it's unlikely that Frosch, Griepentrog, and other settlers could have imagined the controversy that windmills would stir up in their community a century later.

Around 2010—about 130 years after Frosch had put his windmill to work at his cheese factory—a sustainability company based in Chicago presented a polarizing proposal to the quiet countryside of Morrison. They wanted to construct a massive wind farm in Brown County, which included Morrison and the nearby villages of Wrightstown, Glenmore, and Holland. It would be the first of its kind in Brown County and the largest in Wisconsin, with over 100 turbines.

This time, there were no friendly debates about "great enhancements" over drinks at the local tavern. The proposal of towering wind turbines sharply divided the once harmonious town.

The sheer size and number of the proposed turbines—each standing 400 feet tall, compared to the 40-foot windmills of pioneer days—triggered strong opposition from many residents. Concerns included noise, health risks, reduced property values, and fears of water pollution from disrupting the land. Tensions escalated: protest signs filled front yards, some of which were reportedly stolen, and one town meeting ended with a resident accused of pushing a woman.

While the Chicago-based company sought contracts with local landowners, promising lucrative payouts, some residents were outraged at the thought of turbines robbing the community of its idyllic country landscape. In May 2012, a group of Morrison residents filed a federal lawsuit, alleging the town enforced sign ordinances unfairly against anti-turbine activists while ignoring violations by supporters.

In the end, whether all the protests and backlash "worked" is hard to say, but the Chicago-based company eventually stepped away from the project. Still, the memories of this divisive period lingered. Ironically, instead of wind turbines altering Morrison's landscape, it was the signs protesting them that became permanent fixtures along certain roads—lasting reminders of the town's unresolved tensions.

Depending on your point of view, perhaps this vigilance was for good reason. Over a decade later, at the time of this book's publication, new voices are emerging with fresh turbine proposals throughout Wisconsin (as well as other massive, land-altering concepts like data centers)—reviving old questions about how to balance sustainability, profit, progress, health, neighborly courtesy, and the preservation of farmland character.

It remains a complex and emotional debate.

Of course, disagreements in Morrison didn't start with wind power. Nor did dramatic change. The pioneers of the town once cleared sprawling forests and carved out farms—reshaping the land too to suit their own needs and wallets (we discuss this in other chapters).

And, just as today, they gathered to debate the issues shaping their future.

In fact, in the late 1800s, right around the time Frank Frosch's windmill and tavern were notable commodities in Wayside, groups like the Wayside Literary Society met nearby to argue questions that wouldn't sound so out of place today. The Wayside Literary Society became so popular it was said to have made Wayside "famous," hosting spirited debates along with musical performances, readings, and speeches.

Debate topics included the merits of eight-hour workdays, women's suffrage (the girls won this particular debate), and the "disenfranchisement of African Americans in the south." Heavy stuff, right? And, again, not too dissimilar from the ongoing debates, social media groundswells, and catalysts of protest marches throughout future generations.

In pioneer Morrison, these discussions followed a structured format. Each side presented its case in front of judges, in what was essentially a more civil, orderly version of the arguments we see today on all manner of modern screens—without the shouting matches (and hopefully no pushing, either).

Other discussions ranged from playful to profound. Participants debated whether country life was superior to city life, explored whether corporal punishment (presumably the use of spankings and paddles on children in homes and schools) should be abolished, examined U.S. colonial policy and territorial expansion, considered the merits of annexing Hawaii, and, perhaps most vital of all, argued whether or not bachelors should be taxed!

How heated those discussions became (or how much laughter they inspired) is hard to say. But we do know these pioneer-era debates gave people a place to share opinions... and perhaps keep the drama safely on the stage.

If nothing else, it likely fueled better conversation with friends, neighbors, strangers—and maybe even the very bachelors they were debating whether to tax—at the nearest tavern.

Long, Lost Letters & Very Vulgar Phone Calls

Post offices sprouted up across Morrison during its pioneer days, playing a central role in connecting the community. The first post office opened in Morrison in 1859, followed by those in Stark and Wayside in 1869, and Lark in 1893. All are long since gone.

In this bygone era, letters quietly carried stories of war, romance, debts, dreams, forgiveness, and memories to their recipients. There was no technology needed. Just a pen, a willing heart to share thoughts or stories, and time to write them down.

However, on one summer day in 1892, the time it took to write a letter was nothing compared to the remarkable duration it took for it to be delivered.

While stationed in Morrison, Rev. P. Van Susteren penned a letter on August 21, 1892. It was finally received by Rev. M.T. Anderegg in Green Bay on April 8, 1903—nearly *eleven years* later! By the time the letter was unsealed, it was not only an entirely new decade, but a new century as well.

Why there was such a delay, and how the letter survived that long, remains a mystery. Thankfully, the letter was trivial in nature and was of no consequence to either party.

The same can't be said for a letter Alfred Schultz sent in Morrison—or an invitation, to be more precise. In 1904, Schultz mailed a wedding invitation to his aunt, which seemed innocent enough.

But there was one important problem.

Though Schultz had been a respected citizen in Morrison for two years, his past had unsavory secrets. He was wanted in Saginaw, Michigan, for stealing a horse and buggy—and the wedding invitation that he sent in the mail tipped off authorities to his location. He was promptly arrested.

During this same time, communication methods started to evolve with new technologies, but consequences remained part of the equation. While written letters were typically well thought out, penned slowly to choose proper phrasings, phone calls offered a whole different world. With this emerging technology, words could spill out faster and be received instantly.

Not everyone adjusted well to the immediacy of this new tool, and sometimes conversations overflowed with frustrations and a variety of "colorful" words.

In November 1899, the relatively new invention of the telephone found itself at the center of an unusual case involving a young store clerk in Morrison. The clerk, employed by Mr. Saenger in Lark, reportedly used "abusive language" toward George Frosch during a phone call. Whatever words crossed the line, Frosch didn't take kindly to them. It didn't help matters that the clerk refused to retract or deny what he said.

Apparently, these scandalous remarks were so appalling that Frosch marched straight to the authorities, and the offending clerk was hauled into court.

What exactly the clerk said on the phone remains a mystery, but considering the standards of the day, it's safe to assume it likely wouldn't even raise an eyebrow now. After all, the crude vocabulary that today's teenagers use (and the parents they likely learned these musings from) almost certainly exceeds that of the saltiest sailor of 1899. That's a bygone era when "drat!" and "darn!" were a bit daring. Most states had laws against blasphemy, which were defined as taking the Lord's name in vain.

It's also worth noting that telephones in 1899 had an apparatus to speak into and a separate earpiece with a cord, and we have no idea of the quality of sound transmitted in rural areas. Perhaps the young man had to keep repeating what he was saying and lost his temper. Or maybe it was just bad customer service, with tempers flaring in the new world of disembodied voices.

Whatever the cause, the case ended up in front of Justice Thomas Monahan in Wayside. For the justice, this was uncharted territory. The telephone itself was still evolving in small-town Wisconsin. Most rural communities were still figuring out the etiquette of this peculiar device. In fact, the now-ubiquitous "hello" as a greeting was barely catching on.

Given the unusual circumstances, newspapers teased that Justice Monahan was "trembling," nervous that his decision in such a strange case might set a precedent for generations to come. But, in the end, no judgement was needed. Before the trial started, the clerk pleaded guilty, paid a small fine, and returned to his job with (presumably) a lesson in early telephone manners.

Whether anyone else in Morrison's early days was hauled to court for pushing someone's buttons on the phone is unclear; pushing buttons on phones themselves would later become a point of community pride.

By 1968, telephones had come a long way. In Wayside, the local telephone company was preparing for a massive leap forward. At precisely 1:01 a.m. on December 15, the Wayside Telephone Company abandoned its hand-cranked magneto phones and switched to the latest technology: push-button phones. The change wasn't just incremental—it skipped rotary phones altogether.

For decades, customers in Wayside had shared their lines with as many as twelve other households. Every call relied on switchboard operators who manually connected calls. For many, this meant chatting briefly with operators like Cele Suchomel or Gail Schwantes, who were stationed in a village home. Only after this step did they get connected to their actual phone call. Operators worked tirelessly, wearing out three switchboards over 60 years. But with the new system, those shared lines were gone, replaced by one-party lines.

Wayside became the first in the state of Wisconsin and one of just four companies in the entire nation to introduce push-button phones, offering toll-free calls to De Pere and Wrightstown.

The change was monumental for the town. Even the local volunteer fire department felt the impact: the new system could automatically ring every member simultaneously and wouldn't stop until someone picked up—a lifesaving innovation.

With this newly gained ability, Hubert Kiekhaefer, the telephone company's manager, was optimistic about the future. He predicted a world where people could shop by phone, have their purchases delivered, and even pay bills through their bank, without ever leaving home.

While this vision wasn't fully realized with push-button phones, it foreshadowed the revolutionary role technology would later play when phones morphed into high-tech "smart" devices— small enough to be carried around everywhere, and powerful enough to do practically anything.

Now, all manner of tasks and messages can be carried out in real-time on a phone (no eleven-year waits, thank you very much).

In some ways, this brings wonderful advancements. In other ways, it simply creates new complications—as people share their stories of war, romance, debts, dreams, forgiveness, and memories with each other… instantly, and often emotionally.

And, just like before, trouble tends to follow.

After all, from handwritten letters to smartphone screens (to whatever comes next), the problem is rarely how the message is sent.

It's who's sending it.

Painful Progress

Time reshapes everything, and beneath the surface of Morrison's quaint fields and quiet roads, the footprints of those who cleared the land, the sweat and blood that soaked the soil, and the struggles that defined their lives have faded into memory, swept away by the howling winds of progress.

Yet, it's important to recognize the land we build our homes on, the fields that stretch to the horizon, and the roads we cross daily were shaped by the sacrifices of those who came before us.

To do so fully, we must realize how incredibly difficult life could be in those pioneer days.

For the early settlers of Morrison, the land offered great opportunity, but even greater obstacles. Long before vast stretches of corn and crops dotted the landscape, towering forests stretched as far as the eye could see, thick with pines and hardwood.

The transformation of this wilderness into usable farmland came at a cost—of labor, danger, and sometimes life.

The first crop that settlers harvested was timber. Clearing the land was backbreaking work, done tree by tree, stump by stubborn stump. Without chainsaws or heavy machinery, their tools of choice were axes, saws, and dynamite.

The work was so dangerous that trees weren't the only thing being cut away sometimes. For example, in 1897, while at work in a cedar swamp in Morrison, a man had the terrible misfortune of a tree falling on his leg, just below the knee. The tree crushed his leg so badly that amputation was necessary.

When things went more smoothly, logging was a lucrative business. Winters were ideal for hauling logs, as frozen ground made it easier to drag them without sinking into the mud. Sawmills sprang up across Morrison to handle the vast timber supply, turning trees into planks for local and distant markets.

The Branch River was a lifeline for these mills.

Originally known in the early 1800s as the Center River (after Alexander J. Center, a West Point graduate and military surveyor who laid out early roads connecting Green Bay to Fort Dearborn), the more practical name "Branch River" gained favor over time, likely reflecting its role as a tributary of the Manitowoc River.

Regardless of name, it was a monumental resource in clearing the forest. In 1872 alone, the river transported seven *million* feet of pine logs, with the final major pine drive passing through Morrison in 1879.

But, again, clearing this amount of forest was dangerous work, and injuries weren't uncommon. Local sawmills were regular sites of gruesome injuries and deaths. In 1884, a man was struck and killed by a saw at Gross's mill, leaving behind a grieving family. In 1890, a man at Rank's mill lost his arm to a spinning blade. Just under a year later, a boiler explosion at the same mill hurled a young worker into the air, killing him instantly and injuring two others. Beyond these grave threats, fires were also a constant risk. In 1879, a fire in August Haese's sawmill caused $7,000 in damage, while another mill that same year was completely destroyed, uninsured. By the late 19th century, fires at several Morrison sawmills caused thousands of dollars in losses—financially and emotionally devastating for those who depended on them.

Insurance often covered only part of the damage, leaving families to rebuild from scratch.

As hundreds of thousands of trees gradually disappeared from Morrison's landscape, they made way for the open fields we see dominating the town's modern landscape. Pioneer-era farms quickly sprang up to take advantage of this newly cleared land. With it, a huge focus of the community shifted to cultivating crops and raising animals to build a livelihood. Selling milk and cheese (discussed in our next chapter) also became lucrative endeavors. But the risks to early settlers didn't end with this new direction— they simply evolved.

After all, farming has long carried the age-old label of the world's "most dangerous profession."

And for good reason.

Early farmers in Morrison gave horrific examples of this, working without many of the modern safety measures and tools used today. In 1893, Fred Loppnow mangled his arm in a feed cutter so badly it had to be amputated near his elbow. In July 1892, a man unloading hay in Morrison was fatally impaled when a pitchfork fell, piercing his intestines. He died within half an hour but remained conscious until the end. In 1931, another farmer was thrown dozens of feet into the air when dynamite he'd lit to remove a stump exploded beneath him. He was killed instantly.

There was danger in the structures themselves, too.

In 1891, a man in Morrison fell from scaffolding above a barn floor, striking his head on a feed cutter. This resulted in him needing "two half sets of false front teeth for the future." In 1896, a barn being torn down collapsed without warning. One man was instantly killed; another was severely injured beneath the rotted timbers. In 1939, a 65-year-old Morrison farmer fell from a ladder while working in a barn with his son. The collapse shattered his pelvis, possibly fractured his skull, and left him with internal injuries. He was rushed to a hospital in Green Bay in critical condition.

Many more injuries and deaths occurred that never made headlines.

Fires also remained a constant threat throughout Morrison's farming history. An early example in 1896 saw a steam-powered threshing engine ignite a barn fire that destroyed stables, stacks of grain, and livestock shelters, costing over $3,000 in damages. Of course, dozens of other barns and farmhouses went up in flames in future decades—each one marking a difficult chapter for families who saw their livelihoods reduced to ash.

It is worth noting that, to better protect the community from fires, the Wayside Fire Department was organized in 1898 and incorporated in 1900. The Morrison Fire Department followed soon after, beginning in 1905 as a simple bucket brigade before establishing itself formally in 1910. Over the years, hundreds of men and women within these departments have helped families, businesses, and farms in their most dire moments. These guardians of Morrison sometimes paid a price for their service—with hospital stays and, in the grimmest cases, with their lives. Their efforts and sacrifices deserve acknowledgment as well.

Beyond fires on farms, livestock posed their own challenges.

Bulls were notoriously dangerous, and in 1938, a 72-year-old farmer driving cows in from a field near Wayside was crushed and killed by a bull. In 1908, an 83-year-old Morrison woman was gored by a cow, suffering broken hips and internal injuries. She survived for weeks before passing away at home.

Horses, though essential for transportation and farming, were equally unpredictable. A spooked horse could overturn a wagon, throw a rider, or kick with deadly force.

In 1913, a 40-year-old farmer near Wayside was kicked in the head by a horse, fracturing his skull in two places. He died two days later. The kick occurred after the horse was startled by a dog. In 1935, a Morrison farmer was kicked by a cow while milking. He stumbled backward into another stall and was trampled by a horse. Though found alive, he died an hour later from his injuries. In 1900, a woman passing a tied-up wagon on Main Street in Green Bay was kicked in the side by a Morrison man's horse. Her injuries were critical. In another case, a bag of grain fell in 1893, startling a horse and leading to a severe kick to a local man's abdomen.

But animals had their own share of hardship, too.

In modern times, contamination and cows may bring up memories of 2006, when concerns about manure runoff and private wells led the Town of Morrison to pass a new ordinance limiting winter land spreading of manure and other wastes.

But in 1940, it was humans leaving waste that proved unhealthy for their livestock. Six young cattle that year mysteriously died on a Wayside farm. Investigation revealed they had been poisoned by licking an old, discarded five-gallon can of white lead paint in the pasture.

The fences around pastures could be problematic, too. In November 1887, a valuable two-year-old colt on a farm was badly cut and crippled after running into a wire fence. This was just one of many fence accidents that livestock suffered in early pioneer days.

In 1909, the town of Morrison also faced a serious outbreak of rabies when a herd of twenty-seven cattle belonging to William Wedenheft began succumbing to the disease. The trouble began when one cow died in convulsions, and within six weeks, eight more followed. Several veterinary surgeons were called in from around the state, each giving different opinions on what may be the root cause. Finally, a veterinarian questioned the farmer more closely and was able to identify rabies as the issue. The farmer admitted he had killed a dog recently after it was behaving suspiciously on his farm.

Sadly, animal deaths weren't always accidental or from illness.

When the Town of Morrison was just four years old, in 1859, Thomas Morrissy of Maple Grove reported that two of his oxen were shot by someone in the area. One ox returned home with a severe neck wound and had to be put down. While searching for the second, Morrissy found its remains cut into several pieces and buried in the ground, with parts of it sticking out and visible. The gruesome discovery was made on the property of Augustus Teems in the Town of Morrison. The cattle were in excellent condition and likely killed for their beef, prompting Morrissy to take legal action. This disturbing event shows both the value of livestock and the lengths people might go in desperate or lawless times.

Unfortunately, crime and deception cost pioneer farmers in other ways. In 1901, several farmers near Wayside were caught up in an elaborate swindle. The scheme began when men posing as agents of a bankrupt Chicago jewelry company convinced farmers to buy large quantities of discounted watches, supposedly to resell as local agents. A few days later, different men appeared, demanding full payment for the orders.

They threatened foreclosure unless the farmers paid up immediately. In each case, the frightened victims handed over large sums of cash—one nearly $200—in a forced settlement. The fraudsters then destroyed the paperwork and left a few watches behind as supposed compensation. The farmers weren't even sure what they had signed. It was a clever and damaging scheme. (Note: More local crimes, including others involving Morrison farms, are discussed in later chapters.)

For those trying to make a more honest living, farming demanded year-round effort, and many labored well into their 70s and beyond—several of the cases above make that tragically clear.

Yet the youngest members of a household could fall victim, too. In 1889, a 5-year-old girl was killed in a runaway accident on her family's Morrison farm. Her death, though only briefly recorded, is a reminder that danger did not discriminate by age.

And sometimes, heartbreak struck before a young life even had the chance to begin. In 1869, a Morrison man named Mr. Joyce returned home from working in the woods on his farm to discover that his wife had gone into labor while he was away. The baby was already dead, and his wife lay in critical condition. Desperate, he ran to summon help—the nearest neighbor living nearly half a mile away. But when he returned, his wife had died as well. The mother and child were buried in a single grave in De Pere. The couple had been married only two years and had one surviving child. The grieving farmer was left a widower and single parent, his hopes for a growing family shattered in the span of an afternoon.

Simply put, life on the farm was often painful and unpredictable.

A few other examples of this include: A Morrison woman broke her collarbone in 1925 while picking apples in her orchard. In 1934, a 69-year-old man collapsed and died while doing morning farm chores with his son-in-law. And well before that, in 1869, a 45-year-old Morrison farmer died suddenly while lifting a horse that had slipped on Pine Street in Green Bay. It's believed a burst blood vessel caused his death during the strain.

Of course, we'd be remiss not to mention one additional challenge for farmers. As if navigating all the difficulties of machinery and livestock (and crooks) weren't enough, winter storms in Wisconsin are as routine as spring dandelions. Winter often caused additional hardship for pioneer farmers, who had to battle snow and extreme temperatures during their already-difficult tasks.

In 1899, there was a record-setting round of brutal extremes. That year, temperatures plunged to -36°F, freezing cars, closing schools, and making travel impossible.

But the farmers carried on.

In March 1901, temperatures and the bitter wind got so cold in Wayside that a local man said he had never experienced anything like it before. Even wearing furs wasn't enough to block the chill, he said.

But the farmers carried on.

In February 1922, a horrific sleet storm blanketed the community, knocking down 100 percent of the community's phone lines.

But the farmers carried on.

Indeed, despite many hardships, Morrison's settlers always pressed on. By the early 20th century, much of the land had been cleared, and farming took root as the area's defining industry. Dairying grew to prominence, and barns dotted the landscape as symbols of a thriving agricultural community.

The early settlers of Morrison were the agents of progress, carving out a new way of life from untamed wilderness.

One last profound example is the story of a Morrison woman named Mrs. Hickey. She was one of many wives, mothers, and daughters who stood beside men in the community to help face the challenges of the wilderness. She married John Hickey and moved to Morrison in 1855. In the early days, she worked in the fields beside her husband, helping with all manner of haying and harvesting duties. She was also often spotted by neighbors burning piles of logs with him late into the night. When she wasn't assisting him on their farm, she was known for her generosity and care for the sick. In days when no physician could be found nearer than De Pere, Mrs. Hickey frequently stayed several days with those in need without expectation of payment. Due to her admirable work in the community and on her family's farm, her death in 1921 was seen as not only the loss of one of Morrison's last living settlers, but also their way of life.

As one newspaper noted, Mrs. Hickey's death brought "the disappearance of a type of manhood and womanhood which the world will see no more, as the wilderness has been conquered and the frontier is gone forever."

But, as fate would have it, the new ways of life that came after frontier days have largely come and gone too.

Modern residents find themselves victims of new progress, watching as the structures that once defined the town's identity steadily vanish.

The forests that once blanketed Morrison are gone, replaced by fields that now feed fewer families as industrial farming takes hold. Where dozens of sawmills once hummed with activity, only one remains. Many of the barns that once stood as proud testaments to the hard work of Morrison's farmers and families also now stand empty—or have disappeared altogether, just like the towering trees that came before them.

Indeed, the howling winds of progress forever roll onward, and... time reshapes everything.

Say Cheese... & Calamity

In many ways, logging and farming built early Morrison, but cheesemaking helped it thrive.

In the town's pioneer years, this vital industry transformed milk into money, helping farmers survive in a difficult landscape. Roads were primitive, long travel was slow (and sometimes impossible), and milk... well, it spoiled quickly. So, turning milk into cheese was a transformative practice for the community's economic outlook. It allowed Morrison's farmers to preserve their product in a stable, long-lasting form—one that could be stored, transported on treacherous roads, and sold.

For an isolated pioneer town, this was a godsend.

And, in time, it turned out to be incredibly lucrative too, with farmers profiting from cheese sales and deals as far away as Chicago. In fact, at its peak, Morrison had become a regional powerhouse of the cheese industry. The town was home to as many as eight busy factories, producing hundreds of pounds of cheese daily. This local fleet of factories brought in an estimated $30,000 to $40,000 per year in the 1880s alone, the equivalent of over $1 million annually today.

But success carried its own risks. As the town's factories multiplied, so too did the darker side of prosperity: fraud, fines, robberies—and, eventually, tragedy.

72

Crime was an early and frequent visitor. In 1893, an unverified rumor spread that a cheesemaker traveling home from Wayside was flagged down by a man requesting a ride, but after stopping to help—a common courtesy at the time—he was ambushed. Allegedly, two masked men leapt from the roadside, held him at gunpoint, and robbed him of everything he had. Two years later, cheesemakers fell victim to an even bolder scheme, this one easier to verify. In 1895, two men posing as buyers from Chicago struck multiple factories, paying promptly at first to build trust. Then, after receiving a large shipment, they vanished—taking $2,500 worth of Morrison cheese with them. That would be nearly $100,000 worth of goods in today's economy.

Of course, not all problems came from outsiders. Some cheesemakers caused their own trouble. As early as July 1890, Morrison was praised for its excellent cheesemaking, but concerns surfaced about the sanitary conditions of its factories. Some consumers even questioned whether the Board of Health should investigate.

Throughout the years, these concerns were validated on more than one occasion.

A man in Morrison was fined $50 for bringing watered milk to a local cheese factory in 1887. In 1909, a Morrison-area operator was caught running a factory with dirty tools and unsanitary equipment. He pleaded guilty and paid a fine. Just seven years later, in 1916, another factory was cited for similar conditions, with inspectors finding unclean facilities that violated emerging dairy laws. In 1940, inspectors found unsanitary milk being used in production at yet another Morrison factory, leading to yet another fine.

These were just a few of the many citations issued over the years as Wisconsin worked to modernize and regulate its dairy industry. Yet despite the growing pressure for cleaner practices, some operators stubbornly resisted, choosing shortcuts over safety.

Of course, these were isolated problems.

Most local cheesemakers happily abided by regulations and produced many popular products, but it made no difference in the end. By the mid-20th century, Morrison's once-thriving cheesemaking empire was fading, regardless of quality. Changing industry practices, improved roads, and new transportation methods weakened the need for small local operations. Abandoned cheese factories became a common sight—empty reminders of an industry that had once been the heart of the community.

For one of those empty cheese factories—the Stark Cheese Factory—when the steady hum of industry fell silent, a dark cloud quietly rolled in, bringing some of Morrison's most unsettling deaths with it.

In October 1950, beside the old Stark cheese building, two gunshots were fired in one of the town's darkest domestic crimes—a story explored more fully in the next chapter. But even that wasn't the last grim moment tied to a seemingly cursed property.

Just one year later, in May 1951, a new owner of the former cheese factory died in a terrible accident. The 27-year-old man was planning to convert the building into a tire and auto parts shop.

Fate had other plans.

On a spring morning, around 3 a.m., a massive explosion tore through the structure. It's believed that gasoline vapors ignited, causing the accident. Horribly burned, with his clothes still on fire, and in unimaginable pain, the man somehow managed to drive himself over a mile to a neighbor's house. Refusing to wait for an ambulance, he insisted on being driven directly to Green Bay. He died shortly after.

The old cheese factory was also destroyed in the fire.

Now, at the time of this book's publication, none of the eight historic factories remain. Only Laack Bros. Cheese Co. endures as a cheese and butter wholesaler.

The Laack Bros. property, located on Morrison Road, may also represent one final tie to the town's distant past.

Though historical records aren't clear, there's a strong likelihood that Alphonse Morrison and his family—the first settlers of the area and the community's namesake—built their home either on the same land where the Laack facility stands or somewhere across the road from it.

In the end, from those earliest days to the height of the cheesemaking boom, the land around Morrison has seen both beginnings and endings. And while some cheese is said to improve with age, Morrison's industry for it did not. What once sustained its farmers and defined its landscape slowly faded, leaving behind only scattered memories—of prosperity and good future, followed by terrible loss and tragedy.

Murder

"Pa shot Ma!" The words, raw and unthinkable, rang out from the lips of a child seeking refuge at a neighbor's door, signaling a horrific event unfolding in Morrison in October 1950.

Decades earlier, a fugitive from Morrison was also charged with murder after a man was found buried in Michigan under railroad ties.

Needless to say, though the Town of Morrison has remained a peaceful place for most of its history, there have been rare moments when the darkest of violence surfaced. The two known murders above are connected to the town in its first hundred years—leaving uncomfortable scars that time can never fully erase.

The oldest case involves James Brennan, a Morrison man who seemed to live his life on the wrong side of the law. Brennan had already served three years in the Wisconsin State Prison for a robbery committed in the 1890s, among other crimes.

By 1905, Brennan was living in Masonville, Michigan, in a shanty. Near his home, the body of a man named W. W. Dimmock was discovered, buried under a pile of railroad ties. The circumstances pointed to foul play, and suspicion fell on Brennan. Evidence against him was mostly circumstantial, but authorities arrested him and charged him with murder.

The case went to trial in January 1906. The prosecution laid out the details of Dimmock's last movements and Brennan's proximity to the crime scene, but the jury wasn't fully convinced. After deliberating for three days, they returned a verdict of not guilty. Whether Brennan was innocent or simply eluded justice is a question that remains unanswered. What is known is that Brennan seemed to live a deeply troubled life, as did some of the other men he associated with. We'll explore the dark places this led to in one of the final chapters of this book.

Until then, we turn our attention away from this unsolved case with Brennan in Michigan, and revisit another sinister tragedy in Morrison's pioneer era that occurred directly within the town's borders.

By October 1950, the Stark cheese factory had ceased operations and stood abandoned. It was beside this desolate setting that one of Morrison's darkest moments unfolded.

On the evening of Thursday, October 12, a man and his wife—who lived on the property with their four children—had yet another argument in a reportedly strained marriage. But this time, the disagreement turned deadly. When the woman walked away from this latest fight with her husband, things spiraled out of control.

She headed for the front door.

He followed with a shotgun.

"This is your last chance," the man reportedly said... *before pulling the trigger.*

The shot seriously wounded her.

She crumpled to the ground.

Immediately, two of their children fled into a nearby cornfield, terrified he might come after them next. As they ran, they heard a second shot.

The fleeing children eventually reached a neighbor's house, where they told their harrowing story. The neighbor quickly called for help, but it was too late for the father, who apparently turned the gun on himself moments after wounding his wife.

Though the wife survived long enough to recount the tragic series of events, the best efforts of doctors at St. Mary's Hospital in Green Bay could not save her. She succumbed to her injuries days later, leaving her children orphaned and the community reeling from the horrific incident.

Sadly, this wasn't the end of the town's connections to murder.

More than half a century later, with Morrison's pioneer years and this terrible incident long behind it, a chilling discovery took place. It carried sad echoes from both of our previous stories.

Just like someone being buried under railroad ties in Michigan, someone was left murdered and buried in Morrison.

Just like the incident at the town's cheese factory, it appears that marital issues were possibly to blame for a deadly outcome.

And just like those two cases, no true justice ever emerged.

This modern case came to light in 2008, when hunters explored a wooded, marshy area in Morrison. On their quest, they stumbled upon a human skull partially buried in the ground. Alarmed, they contacted the county sheriff, who quickly closed off the area for investigation. Authorities uncovered a complete skeleton, later identified as a 31-year-old woman from Allouez who had been missing since 2003. She had died from a gunshot wound to the head.

Investigators suspected her husband, but he had committed suicide in 2006 while serving time for an unrelated crime. Though the case was considered solved, no one was ever brought to justice.

These three cases—two in Morrison's pioneer years, and one in modern times—remain the most violent crimes tied to Morrison's history, and they are a delicate, uncomfortable thing to revisit. However, their inclusion here is to preserve both *history* and *honesty* with equal reverence.

Because the honest truth is, even in the quaintest of communities, darkness can occasionally seep in.

And so, while we can—and should—celebrate the many people and moments that shaped Morrison in wonderful ways, we also carry the quiet responsibility to remember its most unfortunate victims.

Haunted

The watch lay hidden, year after year, blanketed by earth and mud. The solid gold timepiece had disappeared one afternoon while its owner was picking blackberries in a field. For thirty years, the land was plowed and cleared, the soil churned over countless times, and the watch lay buried and forgotten.

Then, in 1921, a Morrison farmer who now owned the land struck something gleaming while plowing. The internal parts had rusted away, but the case was remarkably well-preserved.

The watch belonged to Dan Falck, a prominent figure in early Morrison history. When reunited with his long-lost watch, Dan may have seen it as more than a trinket—it was a tangible piece of his life that had reemerged from the earth, refusing to be forgotten.

Throughout Morrison's history, there were other times when the past found strange, perhaps even supernatural, ways of lingering and returning.

In 1919, newspapers began reporting strange happenings at the home of Arthur Haese. Built by his father, August Haese, the farmhouse had undergone extensive remodeling after August's death two years earlier. The renovations turned it into what one paper described as "one of the most pretentious residences in the vicinity." But it wasn't long before the house became infamous for more unsettling reasons.

Like scenes from a paranormal movie, the Haese family reported a string of bizarre incidents. Small fires allegedly broke out in the home with no apparent cause. Clothing items stored in chests were shredded to pieces. Pages from a Bible were torn out and scattered. A clock, a centerpiece of the home, was inexplicably broken. The strangest event of all came when the family awoke one morning to find an infant's hair had been completely shaved off during the night.

Rumors of these events spread quickly around town—and beyond.

Soon, local headlines attracted hundreds of curious visitors from around the region to view the house, hoping they could either solve the mystery or, better yet, see something strange and unusual themselves.

Speculation about the cause of these happenings ran wild. Was it August Haese, the family patriarch, expressing displeasure from beyond the grave about the changes to his beloved home? Or was there a more earthly explanation?

Attention turned to an eight-year-old boy in the household, who was even tied to a radiator at one point to keep him from mischief. But when the boy's aunt claimed to see a ghostly hand helping him escape, the mystery deepened.

Arthur Haese fiercely defended his adopted daughter, Ruth, when suspicion shifted to her. Investigators hinted at new leads but never revealed any resolution to the case. By 1926, the Haese family had moved to Manitowoc, leaving the farmhouse behind— and either the mischievous pranks or mysterious hauntings of the dwelling, depending on your point of view.

Elsewhere, another chapter of strange happenings emerged years later, centered on none other than Dan Falck himself. Dan was a charter member of Morrison's fire department. He lived an active life in the community, playing in town bands and sports teams, and was involved in local commerce and church activities until his death on October 13, 1942.

But, much like his watch, buried and forgotten for decades, Dan, too, was said to have resurfaced long after his death—this time in a far more spectral form.

While the Haese farmhouse was seen as a place of odd terror, rumor has it that Dan instead brought a lingering, comforting presence to the tavern he left behind. Originally opened by Dan's father, Phillip Falck, in the 1850s, the tavern became one of Morrison's mainstays. When Dan took it over in 1888, he transformed it, building a new brick structure with an upstairs dancehall in 1895. It was a place of community, celebration, and connection. But, as time passed, it also became a place of eerie fascination for one of its later owners.

In the 1970s, Lloyd Massey bought the building, remodeled, and restored it into the Manor House Supper Club, a German restaurant.

It didn't take long before Massey reported seeing an expressionless man—dressed in white—silently watching him work on the building's renovations… *before fading away*. Massey never described the presence as menacing. He believed it was Dan Falck, still watching over the place he and his family had built.

At least this pioneer "ghost" was polite—something that couldn't always be said for the living.

Massey seemed to face significant resistance and hardship when he purchased and transformed the business. When Massey took over, the building had gone through sixteen owners in ten years. Despite this revolving door of owners, it was seemingly considered a hangout by a few opinionated patrons who resented

Massey's plans to clean it up and turn it into a respectable family dining establishment.

For over a year, while Massey poured significant funds and time into the project, the early morning hours often brought more menacing problems than a friendly ghost.

Rutabagas and other vegetables would come crashing through windows. There were allegedly a few grumbled threats, too, that a fire may someday turn his business into ashes.

But he endured, and so did his business, which became known for its wonderful German cuisine.

However, just as Dan Falck came and went with the passage of time, Massey did, too. And then so did the building itself.

Massey eventually left the Manor House behind in the 1980s, and in 2016, after years of neglect, the Manor House was torn down.

But as legend has it, other modern hauntings continue elsewhere on the property in the building next door (a former general store also originally built by the Falck family). Several claims of paranormal activity in the building have been reported by its current owner, such as the sound of footsteps in the dancehall and chandeliers moving without wind. At one point, this prompted a 2012 front-page Halloween feature in a newspaper in nearby Brillion.

A team of paranormal investigators also came out to explore the space, searching for compelling evidence of the supernatural.

The whispers of Morrison's haunted happenings don't end there. Long after people gathered around the Haese household in the pioneer era to speculate about spooky events, people still gather—online in modern times—to ponder and discuss their own rumors. In 2020, on a popular social media group dedicated to discussing Morrison news and updates, conversation one day turned to the supernatural.

One individual wrote a tale of his son allegedly seeing a ghostly nun resting atop a Morrison church, described as having a bright white face and unnaturally long fingers. The apparent sighting left such an impression that the witness reportedly refused to drive past the church after dark any longer.

And, of course, many sleepovers, backyard campfires, late-night ramblings at taverns, and school recesses have been filled with occasional "ghost story" gossip in Morrison, too.

Whether any of these stories are fact, fiction, or something in between, is up to your point of view and beliefs. Tall tales? Foolishness? Misunderstandings? All fair assumptions. But, perhaps, maybe, just maybe, things always find a way to come back around, whether it's an old watch lying forgotten in the mud, or watchful eyes peering onward from beyond the grave.

Let's Have a Drink

Wisconsin and beer. Need we say more? When German immigrants arrived in the pioneer years, they brought beer-making techniques with them, and soon breweries began popping up like mushrooms after a summer rain. By the late 1800s, Wisconsin was home to over 300 breweries.

But these skilled immigrants didn't just brew frosty pints; they enjoyed drinking them, too. So, just as breweries spread across Wisconsin's landscape, taverns followed closely behind. These taverns served as an oasis for hard-working people to gather, relax, share stories, and enjoy a drink—which was certainly true in early Morrison.

When Phillip Falck opened his general store in 1855, he soon added what is believed to be the town's first-ever tavern next door.

By the time Phillip's son, Dan Falck (the same man discussed in our previous chapter), took over in 1888, the tavern had become a local icon.

Dan rebuilt it with a large, beautiful brick frame, turning it into a hub for political rallies, community dances, wedding showers, business meetings, and a place where many memorable characters quenched their thirst.

One humorous tale from Morrison's "original bar" occurred around 1898. One day, Dan left the saloon in the care of a regular patron—a seemingly trustworthy fellow nicknamed "Mossback."

A newspaper article from the time describes what happened next:

"An old man came in and called for some 'Irish disturbance.' Mossback knew where to find that all right, as he had hit it a few times himself that day. But he gave the man vinegar for a wash, and when Dan returned, the old fellow was still there, making all kinds of faces."

It's a story that may bring a smirk to modern readers; after all, many have likely made "all kinds of faces" during an overly enthusiastic night out. Some of us may also have nicknames for our favorite bartenders or bar patrons (but perhaps nothing as original and unique as Mossback).

Either way, it was clear Morrison's pioneers liked to have fun in their local taverns, but those establishments—and the "fun" they provided—weren't without controversies.

In a young nation still defining its moral landscape, religion played a substantial role, and for many, alcohol represented temptation and vice.

Temperance societies across the country argued that eliminating alcohol would help eradicate social ills. Stories like that of Rose Denny, who was jailed for ten days in 1915 for being drunk and disorderly in Morrison, only strengthened their resolve. Four years after Rose's arrest, temperance activists saw their victory: Prohibition, a federal ban on alcohol, was instituted in 1919.

Prohibition led to the closure of breweries, distilleries, and taverns nationwide. Was this the end for Morrison's bars and characters like Mossback? Not quite.

Some small communities like Morrison continued selling alcohol, despite the risks. Many taverns operated as "soft drink parlors" during Prohibition, advertising non-alcoholic beverages but secretly pouring the real thing for trusted patrons. Despite creative approaches like these, law enforcement wasn't entirely oblivious to the ruse. In 1927, state agents raided three taverns in Morrison, leading to fines for tavern owners Andrew Bornemann, Fred Otto, and, yes, Dan Falck. Each was fined $100—about $1,500 today.

Tragically, a month after the raid, Andrew Bornemann died suddenly at age 41. In his obituary, he was remembered as the owner of a "soft drink parlor," not a tavern, despite the raid just weeks prior.

As fate would have it, Prohibition would have its own end soon after. Congress passed the Blaine Act in 1933, named for Wisconsin Senator John Blaine, repealing Prohibition and allowing citizens to once again enjoy pints openly. Morrison's taverns could finally serve their customers without secrecy, though the end of Prohibition didn't mean an end to occasional trouble.

In 1948, state agents conducted a sweep across the Green Bay area, charging tavern owners for various infractions, from underage sales to prostitution. Two Morrison bar owners were fined for selling beer to minors. In 1950, two other Morrison tavern owners were charged with running illegal dice games, and another near Lark faced allegations of operating a lottery.

Tavern-goers also occasionally found themselves on the wrong side of the law, as one drink too many could lead to fights, accidents, or a night in the county jail.

One particularly colorful example happened in 1938 when an Irish farmer near Wayside "went to town in a big way." After a Saturday night of heavy drinking, likely in Green Bay, the farmer realized early Sunday morning that he'd better return home to milk his cows. Unfortunately, he was in no condition to drive.

Luckily—or so it seemed—he encountered a friendly, portly stranger. The man volunteered to drive the farmer's car and take him home.

There was an obvious flaw with this idea, one that wasn't considered until it was too late. When they arrived at the farm, the stranger wondered how he was going to get back home. The farmer, having not yet tended to his chores, had an equally flawed solution. He politely suggested that they drive all the way back to the city.

The "fun" wasn't over, after all.

Back in town, with cows still not milked, the farmer and the stranger decided to celebrate their return with a drink. Then a few more. Things unraveled further with each new pour. By Monday morning, the farmer awoke in jail "for safekeeping," the stranger was gone, and so was the car. It was later found abandoned on a side street, and the farmer finally drove it home—likely with a pounding headache and a new appreciation for restraint, now believing that "going to town may be all right if you leave out the drinks."

Stories like this remind us that while Morrison's taverns have always offered laughter and community, they've also seen their fair share of misadventures—many of which, thankfully, are better remembered than repeated.

Many other stories of arguments, vandalism, and car accidents have also peppered local newspapers as reminders of the fine line between good-natured fun and foolish (and sometimes fatal) regret.

Over time, many bars came and went, serving Morrison's residents and passing travelers alike. Some of these establishments are now only memories, while others remain local landmarks. For those interested in a historical tavern tour of Morrison, here are a few that still operate (at the time of this book's publication):

In Wayside, the Frosch Brothers sold their business to Maurice Brennan, whose son later opened his own tavern. Frank Pfeffer bought the saloon in 1916, and four bowling alleys were added years later. It's still a popular hangout today, known as The Trading Post, though some may still remember it as Wayside Lanes. Nearby, Frank Frosch built a tavern in 1890, which Fred Pingel soon purchased and expanded with a hotel and residence. The business later became part of Kuntz & Blesser Brewing and today operates successfully as Sally B's Tavern, though some may remember it as DeGreef Ends Here, Riney's, or C&H Corner Bar, among other names. And, another longstanding tavern, first built in 1928 by E.A. Quinnette and Len Detrie, operates now as Tipsy Missy's Bar & Grill. Some older residents may remember it as The Evergreen or The Ponderosa. Finally, there's a bar built in 1890 by Charles Pelischek in the northeastern corner of town. Ownership of this bar has also changed hands many times. Some may remember it as Leiterman's Bar or The Coop, and its current name is Rooster's Coop.

Whether seeking a pint, a laugh, or a bit of local lore, Morrison's taverns have served as community anchors from pioneer days to the present.

For those curious enough to stop by the bars that remain, go ahead and order something tasty (and perhaps vinegar for a wash?), have a good time, find a safe—and trustworthy—ride home, and make whatever faces you'd like.

Scorned Love & Scandals

Morrison's countryside has served as a scenic backdrop for an untold number of first kisses, touching romances, and other passionate encounters throughout its history, not to mention a few weddings.

But, alas, not all romances endure—and not all weddings go as planned, or even happen at all.

Anyone who has suffered heartbreak is probably familiar with the Alfred Lord Tennyson quote: "'Tis better to have loved and lost than never to have loved at all." Though perhaps true, it's doubtful that Bridget Ryan, who was left standing at the altar not once but twice in 1868 by a "well-to-do farmer," would have agreed.

The saga began at a Morrison fair, where John O'Leary, the farmer in question, struck up a friendship with Bridget's father and was invited back to their farm in Maple Grove. Here, a courtship of Bridget commenced. John and a friend he took along enjoyed a warm welcome and lively festivities (and by lively, it appears that alcohol was a primary ingredient in the day's adventure).

By nightfall, after many charming words were showered on Bridget, so intoxicating was the attraction (and the alcohol, presumably), that John and Bridget decided to march to a nearby church and marry the very next morning.

Talk about a whirlwind romance!

But as dawn approached, John sobered up—either literally or figuratively—and his suddenly cold feet didn't feel like marching to a church anymore. The wedding was off.

Well, sort of.

The next evening, after another round of festive cheer and more sweet words whispered from John to Bridget, new vows were planned for the following morning. The couple, back in love, once again pledged their intentions to marry. But before the ceremony could begin, John remembered a rather inconvenient truth: he had a sweetheart back in Massachusetts. By the time the wedding party arrived at the church, John and his friend had quietly vanished, leaving Bridget humiliated and heartbroken.

Newspapers declared: "Faithless John Duped Bridget!" Bridget, however, wasn't about to let him off so easily. Perhaps nothing could mend her broken heart, but money seemed like an appealing way to patch it. She hauled John to court, claiming $1,000 in damages for the "blighted affections and blasted hopes" he caused her (which in today's money would be more than $35,000). Bridget, mind you, felt this price to be quite low.

John, in his defense, argued that even though he "talked swate" to her, no formal promises had been made. A jury of twelve men deliberated the odd case, and ultimately decided Bridget should receive some damages for her trouble, but settled on a sum of $113, which they felt was more equivalent to her suffering.

Speaking of suffering, when the heart is involved, perhaps no emotion triggers more suffering than jealousy. The power of it can unravel even the most stable of lives. Dr. Burke, the town's respected doctor in Wayside (who also caused a dramatic scene boiling a body along the Branch River, which we discussed in our first chapter), was once called upon as a witness in an unfortunate situation of jealousy and perhaps paranoia.

One unfortunate man, who lived in a nearby town, saw his life take a dramatic turn in 1907 after a severe bout of pneumonia. During his recovery, the man became convinced that his wife and brother were carrying on an affair. His paranoia boiled over into threats of violence, as he allegedly vowed to shoot them both— along with the doctor who treated him. Later, the man admitted to owning a revolver but denied making threats. Witnesses, including his wife and brother, testified otherwise. Dr. Burke was roped into testimony due to recently treating the man for his pneumonia. He seemed to feel the gentleman suffered from bouts of illusion and hallucination. The man was the lone person to testify on his behalf.

During his hearing, he appeared calm and reasonable, but a panel of physicians was split on his sanity. They proposed he spend two months in a hospital under supervision.

While the outcome of that stay isn't clear (though one early assessment judged him sane), it appears there was no hope for the troubled marriage. A year later, in 1908, his wife had successfully divorced him, securing $1,535 in cash and property worth $6,000—a tidy settlement for a saga fueled in unknown truths, whether it be fever dreams and rampant jealousy, or legitimate feelings of betrayal.

Ironically enough, Dr. Burke, the respected local physician and witness in the case, was eventually replaced by someone who also caused his share of local marital scandal.

Dr. V.W. Rapp of Wayside became infamous in the early 1920s for his personal and professional failings. A decorated veteran of the British Army during World War I, Rapp's charm couldn't mask his apparent troubles. Reports surfaced that he had practiced medicine without a license, abandoned his wife and their three-year-old child, and that he was fleeing creditors after a series of poor financial decisions.

In November 1922, he telephoned his wife from Fond du Lac claiming he was going far away with a one-way ticket.

His destination: New Orleans, supposedly just a stop on his way to South America. More rumors swirled about his financial woes, including accusations that Dr. Rapp had been traveling in a car encumbered by unpaid debts and that his checks were bouncing left and right. It seemed that, along with his family, creditors were left in his wake.

It's unclear if he was alone on his travels, too.

However, after a six-week disappearance, he returned to Milwaukee. He claimed this was to surrender to authorities, but this is also unclear.

While in a Milwaukee hotel, Dr. Rapp made a phone call to his wife, this time posing as a "friend," perhaps to reassure her of his whereabouts. However, she immediately recognized his voice and alerted authorities. Within thirty minutes, he was in custody.

Back in Green Bay, the doctor faced a slew of charges. His legal troubles culminated in a guilty plea to the abandonment charge, for which he was sentenced to one year in the Green Bay Reformatory. He also faced $3,000 in bail for his other offenses.

Despite his transgressions, there were glimmers of redemption—or at least reconciliation. Dr. Rapp insisted that he had not intended to abandon his family permanently, attributing his departure to the overwhelming debts that he could no longer manage. He promised to turn over a new leaf, stating his willingness to work at any trade to support his wife and child. Remarkably, Mrs. Rapp appeared open to forgiving him and said she intended to take him back. She was a British nurse when they met during the First World War, later leaving her home behind to build a life with him in America. For her to consider forgiving him, after everything, shows a level of devotion—and grace—few could ever match.

Of course, no place in a community preaches forgiveness more than its churches. But even those weren't free from scandals during the pioneer era.

Early on, in 1861, disagreements over doctrine led to the dissolution of St. John's Lutheran Church and the formation of three new congregations. Regardless of the doctrines preached within the walls of these churches, love, loyalty, and possible lust seemed to showcase a wide gulf between the people worshipping and preaching, and the holy life they were striving to achieve.

Take, for instance, an 1874 church trial in Morrison, when Carl Schroeder accused his wife of having an affair with Rev. George Harm of Emmanuel Evangelical Church. The accusation enraged Mrs. Schroeder, who filed for divorce, while Rev. Harm sued Carl Schroeder for $5,000 in damages.

Perhaps cooler heads and forgiveness ruled here as well.

Schroeder and his wife reconciled, withdrew from the divorce, and went on another honeymoon. Schroeder also claimed that he did not actually speak the words for which he was being sued for, and eventually a jury cleared him of this liability, while also clearing the minister of any wrongdoing.

Roughly a half-century later, another minister found himself in the crosshairs of a man in his congregation also making bold claims.

This peculiar scandal in 1920 was linked to a man named Frank Gruett. It is presumed, though not confirmed, that this Gruett was likely the same individual who served as the first resident teacher at Morrison Zion Lutheran School in 1886. We include it here due to its potential tie a notable figure in Morrison history, but realize it may be unrelated. Regardless, the matter still stands as an example of small-town drama and scandal in our region.

By 1920, it appeared Gruett had relocated to Rosendale, where he clashed with Rev. Gerlach of Rosendale Lutheran Church. Gruett accused the pastor of scandalous behavior, though modern perspectives might interpret some of his claims as more eccentric than egregious.

Gruett claimed that Rev. Gerlach had been spotted eating ice cream at a local function while lying on his stomach with his "hind legs in the air" and, horror of horrors, dancing the two-step. Some were unphased, claiming that if the pastor had attempted the "shimmy" or the "houtchy-koutchy," there might have been more cause for concern—but not the graceful two-step! But things only escalated when the minister, upon being noticed by Gruett's wife, held up a finger and said, "pst," further souring the Gruetts' view of him.

But the ice cream escapade was just the tip of the iceberg.

Gruett compiled a long list of alleged offenses, ranging from the seemingly trivial to the potentially serious. The pastor was accused of "acting up before three old maids" at a local post office, shaking his clenched fist in Gruett's wife's face during a disagreement about the congregation's women's society (and causing her daughter to flee the church in fright), advising a troubled parishioner to find solace in brandy rather than scripture before a surgery, and even having his fortune told in a Rosendale store. Perhaps the most serious accusation was that the minister had fathered an illegitimate child with a local telephone operator.

Not content to keep his grievances within the congregation, Gruett took his allegations to the president of the Iowa Synod, accusing the church of whitewashing the pastor's alleged misconduct.

Whether the disgruntled Gruett's claims had any basis is hard to determine, but his public airing of grievances would ultimately lead to his own consequences.

The escalating accusations culminated in a slander suit filed by Rev. Gerlach, who argued that Gruett's letters to Lutheran ministers across Wisconsin were driven by malice. The trial drew large crowds, eager to witness the proceedings.

In the end, the jury sided with Rev. Gerlach, awarding him $5,000 in damages to repair his tarnished reputation—half the amount he sought.

However, it was still far more than poor Bridget Ryan received in Morrison decades earlier, when she tried... unsuccessfully... to mend her twice-broken heart.

Chaos, Crime, & Comedy

The state of Wisconsin covers about 65,000 square miles. Of this, the Town of Morrison accounts for just under 37 square miles.

Tiny place? Absolutely. Tame? Not always.

The people who settled this tiny pioneer town were no less flawed than those in larger communities—and the town's early history was occasionally marked by flashes of chaos, crime, and comedy as a result. The preceding chapters have highlighted this well, touching on many curious tragedies and humorous mishaps. But here, we look at another series of infamous events that shaped Morrison's pioneer years.

In the fall of 1883, burglars broke into Phillip Falck's home, cracked his safe, and stole $110 in cash. Earlier that year, overnight thieves targeted two businesses. At Jacob Falck's store, they drilled a hole in the safe and prepared a powder fuse to blow it open, but the sound of footsteps on the stairs scared them away. At John Hahn's business, they managed to break the safe but not the money drawer, again fleeing when frightened off. In 1898, burglars broke into the home of Maurice Brennan and stole $500 in cash and $95 in gold, slipping away undetected while the family was asleep. In 1914, George Frosch's safe in Wayside was also blown open with dynamite, scattering checks across the floor. Thieves made off with $300.

Fast forward a few decades to October 1931—an even more daring crime was attempted in Wayside. This time, robbers approached the Wayside State Bank armed with acetylene torches, intent on breaching its vault. They had prepared meticulously, even stealing large milk cans to fill with water as a precaution against fire. Breaking in through a side window, they burned through the outer and inner vault doors, eventually reaching a smaller interior compartment.

Yet their grand prize—a large safe containing thousands of dollars in cash—eluded them. As they worked, it's believed that passing youths returning from a nearby dance frightened the robbers away. They fled with a modest haul of $211.60 in coins and a Colt revolver, leaving behind burned vault doors, discarded tools, and empty milk cans.

In 1946, another incident in Morrison reached a new low in common decency. A robber took advantage of a crippled farmer, breaking into his home at night. The intruder blew out a bedroom lamp, tied the man to a bed, and stole more than $1,000. Then he slapped the farmer several times and disabled the telephone before fleeing. It's unknown if the culprit was ever caught.

While money was often on the minds of thieves, there were other targets as well.

In 1882, several horses were stolen from a farmer's stable.

In February 1888, another man stole a horse and cutter in Fort Howard but was spotted and captured in Morrison.

In 1935, two bill collectors went to Mrs. Anna Fenion's farmhouse. When no one answered the door, one grabbed a chicken to draw her out. The men left with two chickens and were later charged with theft. In 1937, a pair of Morrison farmers stole four heifers from a nearby farm. The two men were sentenced to terms of one to two years in state prison at Waupun. In 1940, a wave of chicken rustling swept through Morrison, with dozens of birds disappearing in a single night. The culprits were never caught.

Elsewhere in the town, when animals weren't victims of theft, they were sometimes used to deter it. But the following example seems like a rather trivial moment to warrant any precautions.

In August 1890, an elderly Morrison man apparently believed a group of four little girls and a woman picking blueberries were trespassing on his property, so he followed them with a pitchfork and two "fierce growlers" [likely referring to a pair of dogs]. He claimed he merely had his growling beasts there to keep an eye on things. No need to attack anyone, he assured.

Naturally, he was an old man the little girls developed a healthy dislike for.

On a much more serious note, violence was another ongoing reality for early pioneers. In November 1865, a German immigrant named Mr. Kuntz was attacked while walking home at night. Knocked unconscious, he survived only because his cries for help frightened off his attackers.

Three years later, in December 1868, arsonists burned Michael Quinn's barn to the ground—a crime blamed on itinerant workers, or "tramps," who sometimes retaliated against farmers unwilling to offer food or shelter.

Quinn was the first-ever town clerk and justice of the peace in Morrison and was described as a man of integrity and intelligence. But, after his farm burned to ashes, it was said that "trouble beset him on every side" and "nothing seemed to prosper in his hands."

Discouraged and heart sick, Quinn apparently sold his farm and moved away. Rumors state he died within a year of leaving town.

In 1870, another man was assaulted in Morrison. His ribs were broken, and he suffered internal injuries so severe that local physicians feared he would never recover from them.

In 1915, an apparent fight in Morrison with three men from the Oneida tribe left one man severely beaten by clubs.

Fraud occasionally surfaced, too, as it did in 1877 when John Gross, a justice of the peace, was charged with forging the signature of a woman who could neither read nor write English. His trial attracted plenty of local attention. In August 1887, a woman was arrested after convincing merchants she was creditworthy by claiming to own a debt-free 160-acre farm. She amassed $600 to $700 worth of goods before disappearing with the money.

Numerous swindlers were also active at the Morrison Fair in October 1887. There, they cheated visitors out of $5 to $15 each. A prominent De Pere businessman was said to be aiding the scheme by "baiting the suckers."

Yet outsiders weren't always taking advantage of Morrison residents.

In 1891, Morrison's Mike Flaherty lost a pocketbook containing $800 while driving from Morrison to De Pere. Luckily, it was found and returned by Herman Trapp of Cooperstown. Trapp received a reward for his honorable deed.

To put his actions in perspective, it was the equivalent of stumbling upon nearly $30,000 in today's money, yet returning it to its rightful owner.

Beyond scams and violence, pioneer life—especially travel—was perilous in its own right.

Roads were so rough that some Morrison men even went west to help build better ones. In 1890, Thomas Conniff of Morrison supervised construction of a section of the government stage road in Yellowstone National Park, a job that brought him into the heart of a young national treasure.

Back home in Morrison, however, roads received far less attention and resources. Building them was difficult and tedious. Driving on them wasn't much better. In a time before automobiles, residents guided wagons and sleds slowly over rugged terrain, often carrying heavy loads.

And when things went wrong, they went terribly wrong.

In February 1859, one of Morrison's most active farmers, Mr. Howard, sat atop a pile of saw logs. While descending a hill, the sleigh broke, and the massive logs tumbled onto him, crushing him to death. He left behind a wife and several children.

In her diary, Martha Lemke, who grew up in Morrison in the late 1800s, also recalled a dangerous incident on a hill. This moment left behind children in a different (less tragic) way. While riding in a buggy with her family, the rear seat suddenly slipped off. She and her brother were thrown backward, landing hard in the road, still sitting in the seat itself. "The way we went down backwards, I am surprised we didn't get hurt more," she wrote, adding "We must have been made of rubber."

On already lousy roads, winter brought even more trouble, including a terrible storm that caused an unusual accident in February 1885.

A Morrison farmer was delivering cattle in Fort Howard. His livestock were being put in the yard for shipment when blinding snow caused chaos. A plow ran into the drove of 42 head of cattle and killed eight. In these whiteout conditions, the engineer was completely unaware of what he'd done until he reached an area near Duck Creek. There, one of the oxen that was carried along by the plow finally fell off. It landed on the tracks and derailed the engine.

While this odd incident is one that literally nobody saw coming, the same can't be said for another accident in 1878. That tragedy saw Philip Purr driving a load of hay into town with his wife and baby. Sensing an unsteady load, Mrs. Purr voiced concerns to her husband. He dismissed them, telling her in no uncertain terms that she didn't know what she was talking about.

While a man brushing off his wife's "driving advice" is a tale as old as time, Mr. Purr's decision to ignore his wife proved tragic on this occasion.

Just moments after expressing unease, his wife was thrown from the wagon, along with her child. Thankfully, both were miraculously unharmed. Mr. Purr, however, was less fortunate. He was tossed onto the road, crushed under the wagon's wheels, and killed instantly.

In 1887, James Clark also had a mishap with his team of horses. He fortunately wasn't killed but did suffer several injuries, including a broken jaw—and a little insult to injury, too. He had been riding with a hired hand when the accident occurred. Instead of checking on his injured boss, who was resting at a neighbor's house, the hired man went to Clark's home and stole $64. He was later arrested, already having spent $40.

Among the lighter stories of pioneer travel is an instance where someone made money, not lost it, due to rough road conditions. Knowing how difficult the journey was, a man accepted a wager in 1888 that he couldn't travel from Morrison to Green Bay... and back... in six hours.

Despite the primitive roads, he surprisingly pulled it off. On roads that were little more than rutted paths, that was no small accomplishment.

For comparison, using modern vehicles and roads, a similar roundtrip today by car would likely take an hour or less.

A different man in early Morrison also garnered attention for long journeys. Not because of their speed, but because he could make them at all.

That popular figure was named Joseph St. Thomas. In 1886, he was an elderly resident said to be ninety-nine years old, yet feeling no older than forty. In fact, as he approached his 100th birthday, he allegedly could still walk twenty to thirty miles in ten hours "with perfect ease."

Unfortunately, while Thomas enjoyed a spry life well into old age, elsewhere in Morrison, some of its youngest residents had their lives tragically cut short. Many times, this was simply due to freak accidents or misfortune.

A few somber examples include:

In June 1891, a young boy from Morrison lost his life in a baseball-related accident. The boy, the son of Jerry Brennan, was running with a bat in hand when one end of it struck a fence, driving the opposite end into his stomach with fatal force.

The next summer, in July 1892, an eight-year-old boy fell into a creek while boating with friends. Though he was rescued and returned home, he was later seized by cramps and died a few hours later.

In November 1889, a tragic accident occurred when a two-year-old girl fell backward into a pot of boiling lye that had been placed on the floor after soap-making. She died from her burns shortly after.

Guns, too, played an unfortunate role in the town's tragedies. In 1876, a young man hunting in the woods accidentally shot himself when his rifle's hammer struck a branch. The bullet passed near his heart, and he died within hours.

Five years later, in 1881, another man suffered a similar fate when his hunting partner's weapon discharged while tangled in willow branches. He died within fifteen minutes.

Revolvers, increasingly common in the late 19th century, also introduced new risks. In 1882, yet another man from Morrison was accidentally shot when a companion carelessly played with a loaded gun.

The incident fueled public frustration, and a local newspaper railed against the "senseless young men" who carried revolvers, questioning both their judgment and the need to flaunt weapons. Even in Morrison's early days, debates over gun safety and regulation were already taking shape.

And yet, additional gun-related deaths and accidents sadly occurred in the decades that followed, mostly stemming from more hunting mishaps.

Of course, like so many moments in Morrison's past, these incidents were soon overshadowed by new misadventures and the next round of chaos waiting to unfold.

But one gun-related story stands apart—a riveting tale of chaos, crime, and... *consequences* that we'll unravel in our next chapter. It highlights a violent episode in Morrison that sent shockwaves through the young community and sparked a dark manhunt, driving the culprits far beyond the town's quiet borders and straight into the shadows of infamy.

The Final Curtain

It was over. The lights of the Dreamland Theatre went out for the last time in Wayside in the 1950s. The crowd that had gathered scattered away like leaves in the wind. *There was nothing left to see.*

So ended decades of laughter, music, and make-believe on Morrison's small-town stage.

Dreamland had been a proud little theater in its day. Built in 1913 by the Wayside Amusement Company, it was once a community treasure—a gasoline-powered marvel with an orchestra pit and velvet curtains, where local families gathered to see the world brought to life on stage. Traveling troupes and homegrown performers presented every kind of story: romance and farce, mystery and morality, comedy and crime.

A few of the plays, among dozens that were featured in Morrison through the years, included Go Slow, Mary (1925), Climbing Roses (1930), Who Wouldn't Be Crazy? (1933), and Father Goes on a Diet (1951).

One popular production about crime and redemption was staged in May 1924. The play, Tony, the Convict, had been featured all around the country for years. On Dreamland's stage, it was performed with pride by a local cast. The story followed a man newly released from prison, trying to find his footing in a world that no longer trusted him. It was a humorous tale of guilt, forgiveness, and the fragile hope of redemption.

The play itself had been written three decades earlier, in 1893, by Charles Townsend.

As fate would have it, that same year—1893—a few men in the Town of Morrison were writing a very different kind of drama.

Their stage was an unsuspecting farmhouse instead of a theater. Their lines were vicious threats, not humorous dialogue. And their story would not end with a crowd applauding, but with people gathered for something far darker.

So, what happened? Well, take a seat and settle in—at least in your mind—just as those early audiences once did at Dreamland, and listen to a story, a true one, about a notorious gang from Morrison's distant past.

(Cue the curtains.)

It began with a dog barking in the quiet of a summer night—a sound that hinted at trouble, though its meaning was unclear.

On that fateful August 1893 evening, F. C. Saenger, a general store owner in Lark, went outside to investigate what was bothering his faithful four-legged friend. Seeing nothing, he dismissed the noise and prepared for bed. But about an hour later, there came a knock at the front door. When he answered, a visitor handed him what he claimed was a telegram.

As Saenger took the paper, the stranger crashed through the door—followed by two masked men.

In the blink of an eye, Saenger found himself staring down three revolvers. One of the men pressed his gun snugly against Saenger's head.

"Old boy, I've got you. Throw up your hands or I'll shoot," he ordered.

Saenger complied as the men tore through the house, seizing cash and valuables but growing increasingly frustrated when they suspected more money was hidden. After all, Saenger wasn't just a postmaster and storekeeper—he also owned a cheese factory, and, as we know from earlier chapters, that was a lucrative business in pioneer days. Some reports even stated that Saenger's operation was one of the most successful in the state.

The robbers grew angrier, tearing up important papers while ransacking the home. They threatened again to use deadly force if they weren't shown where the rest of the money was hidden.

Saenger called to his wife and wished her a nerve-wracking goodbye. Meanwhile, he slyly slipped her a key to the drawer where the money was kept. Perhaps he hoped to create a distraction—a brief window of time where his wife could get away, save their funds, and escape without him. No such luck.

The burglars caught on and prevented her from moving. Next, they escalated their threats.

The criminals said they would kill the entire family if the hiding place of the money was not revealed within three minutes.

Saenger had no choice but to give in.

After showing them the drawer, the trio made off with about $1,400 in cash—most of it meant for the employees of Saenger's cheese factory—along with two gold watches and a revolver. Before escaping, they marched Saenger into the darkness, one masked man on each side holding an arm while the third walked behind, revolver still leveled at his head. At last, they released him far enough away to secure their getaway.

The robbery shocked Brown County. The intruders had carried themselves with a boldness rarely seen in rural Wisconsin. Local farmers were so appalled they chipped in for reward money, hoping it would lead to a quick arrest.

Of course, on a stage in a theatre, crime stories usually lead to justice or redemption. In this real-life drama in Morrison, both were far more elusive.

At first, there were no solid leads. Then reports surfaced that three men had stopped at Philip Sherlock's home in De Pere, asking Mrs. Sherlock for something to eat. While she prepared a meal for them, the men stepped outside and left behind a satchel. Suspicious of their behavior, she opened it and found several revolvers and knives. When they returned, she asked one of them if his name was Brennan. In fact, she insisted it was, though he denied it. Instead of staying to eat, the men departed immediately. Mrs. Sherlock later said she believed one of them was James Brennan, though his face had been partially masked and she could not be certain.

Either way, this information was enough for authorities to turn their attention to James and Timothy Brennan—twin brothers from Morrison—and a slippery young man named Henry Cingmars.

Cingmars, sharp-eyed and restless, lived near Wrightstown. Only in his mid-20s, he was already whispered about as "one of the smoothest criminals who ever operated around Green Bay." The Brennans were local Morrison farmers and no less notorious. They were described as "always of a daring character." James, in particular, had a knack for finding trouble.

The year before the Saenger robbery, James had already stolen eleven head of cattle in Green Bay. He sold the cattle to a butcher under an assumed name—Dan Donohue of Glenmore. When investigators went to Glenmore to confront him, they discovered they'd been deceived: the real Dan Donohue was not the culprit and James was long gone.

Rumors said that James fled to Oklahoma for a few months to escape punishment. While there, legend goes that James Brennan indulged in a "wild and reckless life" and became a dead shot with his revolver. He was also in his mid-20s, strong, with a black moustache and an abundance of confidence.

He was considered crafty and dangerous.

Nonetheless, two weeks after the Saenger crime, investigators closed in.

It was discovered that the Brennan boys and Cingmars were spotted in Rhinelander—enjoying a show in a theatre, of all places. After arriving in town, investigators learned that James Brennan had deposited a wad of suspicious cash with a saloonkeeper. This was later identified as Saenger's stolen payroll.

Beyond that, there was no trace of the trio. The trail went cold again… until a woman revealed she had recently spent time with James Brennan in a nearby village.

How the woman fit into James's "wild and reckless life" is unclear, but authorities waited patiently, staking out Rhinelander until he returned to see her again.

When he did, Sheriff Ed Gaffney arrested him and brought him to Green Bay for trial.

That didn't mean he had any intention of serving time behind bars. Before his appearance in court, in October 1893, James Brennan and another prisoner made a daring attempt to escape from their jail cell. When a guard unlocked a door to secure the prisoners for the night, the pair suddenly dashed out before it could be closed again. The other inmate ran into a nearby room and leapt through a window, falling twenty feet but successfully escaping.

Brennan, meanwhile, ran down the stairs into a kitchen. The guard followed in fast pursuit. Brennan might have escaped as well, had he not crossed paths with another prisoner named Henry Bartenschlock. Instead of letting him pass through or aiding his getaway, the fellow prisoner wrestled him to the ground. Enraged, Brennan punched him in the face in an effort to break free, but it was no use. Bartenschlock was left with a black eye but received public praise and encouragement that he receive "credit" for his help.

When Brennan's court date finally arrived, the case drew intense interest. The courtroom was packed as Saenger testified about the traumatic robbery. In the end, James Brennan was found guilty and sentenced to three years in Waupun Prison.

While James was stuck in prison, his accomplices were still on the run.

Timothy Brennan and Henry Cingmars were questioned briefly in Minneapolis at one point but released, which greatly frustrated authorities back in Morrison. Eventually, for unknown reasons, Timothy returned to Morrison a couple years later to live quietly on the family farm. How he avoided charges remains unclear.

Cingmars, meanwhile, kept finding creative ways to slip through the grasp of justice. Rumors said he had relatives in Rhinelander, including the city marshal, who may have helped his initial escape. From there, it was suspected that other bribes and connections helped Cingmars stay one step ahead. Each time Sheriff Gaffney followed a lead—to Minneapolis, Iowa, Texas, and back toward Rhinelander—he found only footprints cooling in the dust.

With nowhere to run, James Brennan served two and a half years of his three-year sentence before being released for good behavior—but with a catch. His past had already caught up with him. The cattle he stole from Mrs. Augustine Henry in 1892 was a matter unresolved. When James's prison term ended for the Saenger robbery, Sheriff Delaney met him at the gate with a fresh warrant and new cuffs. He was then charged with obtaining money under false pretenses and larceny for the 1892 cattle case.

It appears that James stayed in jail for another two years for this older crime.

In Townsend's fictional play performed at Dreamland Theatre, the lead character's time behind bars was a turning point—a chance for redemption. For James Brennan, his real-life stint in jail was simply an intermission from his wild and reckless life.

By 1903, James was out of jail, and the Brennan brothers were back together in Morrison. It didn't take long before they were reunited with trouble, too. That year, they were accused of passing counterfeit silver dollars during Fourth of July festivities in Denmark.

During that fateful evening, a bartender grew curious about their identity. He thought they were from the Brennan family and wanted to know their first names.

Instead of giving answers, they curtly replied that "Brennan is enough."

That wasn't enough for federal agents, who came from Milwaukee to make arrests. James and Timothy Brennan found themselves sitting in a courtroom soon after. In an odd twist, their defense attorney was the same man who had prosecuted James a decade earlier for the Saenger robbery.

Luckily for them, the twin brothers' similar appearances made witness testimony unreliable, and there wasn't enough evidence to convict them of the counterfeiting scheme. After five hours of jury deliberation, Timothy Brennan was acquitted. He sat stoically as the verdict was read. But James couldn't hide his relief. Reports say a dark flush came over his face as he realized his twin's verdict likely meant he would share an identical fate. He was right.

Shortly after, James was acquitted, too.

But unfortunately, even this close call didn't push James toward a path of redemption.

Just two years later, in 1905, he was again suspected of a crime—this one far more serious. James was charged in Michigan for what was described as the most "brutal murder ever recorded in Delta County."

This is the same case we briefly mentioned earlier in the "Murder" section of this book.

As you may recall from that chapter, the victim was W. W. Dimmock, a traveling agent from Milwaukee. Someone had crept up behind Dimmock and fired a fatal shot into the back of his head before burying his body beneath a pile of railroad ties. Brennan was seen with Dimmock the night before, and suspicion quickly fell upon him. When authorities confronted James, he fled, leading investigators on a two-hour chase. When he was finally caught, he gave yet another false name—John Jones, this time. He insisted this was his true identity until several hours of intense questioning left him cornered. At last, he gave in and admitted his real name was James Brennan. He also disclosed his prior time in Wisconsin state prisons, but denied having anything to do with the Dimmock murder. If innocent, why Brennan felt the need to flee and give another alias is unclear, but regardless, a jury ultimately found him not guilty of the crime, feeling the evidence was mostly circumstantial.

James Brennan may have been a troublemaker and a "dead shot" with his revolver, but probably not a murderer, the law decided.

After this harrowing ordeal, the Brennan brothers' story seemed to fade. What became of them afterward is uncertain. Records appear to show that James Brennan passed away sometime in 1907, which would have been only two years after his murder trial. In newspaper notices from that year, it looks like Timothy was applying to become administrator of his brother's estate. Meanwhile, Timothy appears to have died in 1931 at the age of sixty-three.

And now, please remain comfortably in your seat. The story doesn't end there. Our dramatic grand finale is about to commence.

As for the Brennans' old associate, Henry Cingmars—his final act took place far from Morrison, just a few years after the Saenger robbery.

The sly young criminal was known as a good dresser, wearing diamond shirt studs, scarf pins, and a thin moustache. In his underclothing, he always carried a large sum of money sewn in, and once drunkenly boasted that he had at least $1,800 ready to "buy any turkey in the country." In today's money, that would be roughly $65,000 in bribery cash.

Clearly, Cingmars thought he was above the law. But in the summer of 1896, everything changed.

The dangerous behavior that had long defined Cingmars' life reached its boiling point. With James back in Wisconsin serving jail time, and brother Timothy fleeing the law elsewhere, Cingmars apparently found a new partner in crime named Dorman Musgrove.

The two had been acquainted for about three years, having logged together near Rhinelander. Linking up with Musgrove was a fatal mistake.

Ironically, it all started, once again, with the barking of a dog.

According to their own testimony, on June 24, 1896, Henry Cingmars and Dorman Musgrove were on their way toward Mankato, hoping to find harvest work farther south. They had spent days wandering, and by the time they were six miles outside Glencoe, Minnesota, a farmer with a wagon came up the road and offered them a ride. They accepted.

The farmer had a large mongrel dog with him.

For a while, the journey was uneventful, until another stray dog suddenly rushed out from a field. Without hesitation, the stray canine clamped on to the farmer's dog, biting and "chewing him up," as Musgrove later put it. The wagon's farmer cracked his whip to drive the stray off, and though it scampered back toward a field, it returned again moments later and attacked the farmer's dog a second time.

Allegedly trying to help, Musgrove fired his gun in the direction of the dog. He insisted he fired a single shot into the ground only to break up the attack—that he never meant to hurt anything.

Whether or not that was true, the gunshot changed the mood instantly.

The stray pooch yelped and ran back toward a man plowing in the nearby field. The man stopped and went to investigate what was bothering his faithful four-legged friend.

At that point, things took a darker turn. The wandering Wisconsin men found themselves facing criticism for their actions. It's unclear whether it was the farmer in the wagon or the plowman in the field who took offense (*it was most likely the plowman*), but one of them became irritated about the gunfire and accused the pair of shooting at horses.

Cingmars—a man who apparently didn't handle tension gracefully—also became irritated.

Everything spiraled from there.

Quick-tempered and impulsive, he slapped the complaining farmer across the face, knocking his hat to the ground. He then picked up the fallen hat, shoved it back toward the man, and told him sharply to mind his own business.

The farmer hurled insults of his own, and Cingmars, unable to leave well enough alone, struck him two or three more times, knocking him down again. The man rose, brushed himself off, put on his hat, and stormed about twenty feet up the road before turning back and shouting that he'd "have the law" on them for this.

It's worth noting that different accounts of this confrontation claimed that the farmer was not only beaten… but also robbed. Meanwhile, other reports claim it was Musgrove, not Cingmars, who became aggressive.

No matter which version is true, "the law" was soon on its way.

Officials gave chase in a horse and buggy and jumped from it when they spotted their two suspects. Instead of surrendering peacefully, things spiraled even further out of control.

Once again, what happened next depends on whose account you believe.

The two outlaws both claimed that Sherrif Joseph Rogers reached for his gun first, escalating the situation. The fugitives claimed that Cingmars' reached for his gun next to demand time to explain their side of the story, but it went off by mistake. This "accidental" shot struck the sheriff, piercing him near the wrist. Meanwhile, a different telling of the showdown suggested that Cingmars was simply trying to shoot the gun out of the sheriff's hand, but the lawman's erratic movements caused him to miss his mark.

Either way, it was the next shot fired that changed everything.

Like Cingmars, Musgrove said he was merely defending himself when he saw the Sherrif reach for his gun. According to Musgrove, it was a "case of the sheriff either shooting me or I the sheriff, and I got the drop on him. If he had not reached for his gun, I would not have shot." In other words, he felt the sheriff was about to kill one of them, or both, and Musgrove was simply acting in self-defense. But other reports paint a different picture. Those recaps say that when Sherrif Rogers informed the pair that he wanted them to return to Glencoe with him, Musgrove defiantly raised a Winchester rifle and replied, "Well, we don't have to go," before firing and shooting the sheriff in the chest.

What truly happened leading up to that moment is hard to say, but the outcome was crystal clear. In the blink of an eye, Cingmars' new partner in crime had shot and killed the sheriff, raising the stakes considerably for their life on the run.

The warrant for their arrest was found later in the sheriff's pocket—pierced by the bullet that killed him.

The story swept across the region like wildfire. Sheriff Rogers was well respected in the area. Alarms sounded in towns all around Glencoe and search parties formed instantly. Angry citizens flocked together to hunt down the fugitives, driving them relentlessly through fields and swamps over the next nineteen hours. Exit roads in the area were blocked off or monitored. In all, groups from at least seven towns swept over the region, combing land in a 30-mile radius from the place of the murder.

As the search wore on, it became abundantly clear: the killers could slink around the countryside all they wanted, but they weren't getting away.

The search parties got their big break about ten miles from the scene of the murder. A farmer wanting to help climbed his windmill and noticed two men in his fields. He signaled to those searching for the bandits, helping them narrow their search. Cingmars and Musgrove then tried to hide in tall reeds by a lake but were quickly surrounded. Some reports say that Musgrove and Cingmars entered the water and submerged themselves up to their chins, trying to hide from view. But scanning the reeds, someone spotted a hat and fired a shot over it.

This first shot likely came from one of Sherrif Rogers' dearest childhood acquaintances, Mark Carstens. Carstens was brokenhearted while leading his search party, his eyes burning red with tears while trying to avenge the death of his fallen friend.

After Carstens' shot, more men lifted their guns. Soon, bullets rained down, peppering the water fiercely around the fugitives.

The criminals had no choice but to surrender. They walked out from the water unarmed, before being led to wagons, shoved inside, and driven back to Glencoe.

The elusive criminal who had once pointed a revolver at F. C. Saenger in Morrison was now finally in custody.

And his arrest was nothing short of a spectacle.

It didn't take long for roughly 1,000 people to gather near the Glencoe jail. The town's mayor ordered that all saloons be closed for the remainder of the day. This was an attempt to keep alcohol and vengeful emotions from igniting into a deadly combination, but many residents angrily shouted for the prisoners to be lynched anyway.

As the fury started to mount, the acting sheriff, city attorney, and mayor of Glencoe were so overwhelmed that they sent a telegram to the governor of Minnesota seeking reinforcements. A militia was sent to help protect the prisoners. Still, things grew so intense that the criminals eventually had to be transported to St. Paul to deescalate the situation and await trial.

Their train ride to St. Paul was another demonstration of how serious the situation was.

Anyone entering the locomotive had to show credentials. Beside Cingmars and Musgrove sat the acting sheriff and justice of the peace. Surrounding them on the train were forty-eight members of Company D of St. Paul, all dressed in uniform and armed with weapons.

Clearly, any money stashed away to weasel out of jail wouldn't work this time.

After the train arrived in St. Paul, reporters spoke with the criminals. Cingmars sat quietly, wearing a large felt sombrero, overalls, dark-colored shirt, and a scowl. Far from his home in Brown County, this made an instant impression, and it wasn't a good one.

One reporter said "Cingmars was undoubtedly the most villainous looking of the two." He noted that Cingmars' "large and dark brown" eyes were piercing and "when he looks at a person, he looks with a cold, hard and cruel stare and a sneer voluntarily appears."

When the same reporter asked him for his version of events, the former Morrison criminal was defiant. "I guess I've nothing to say; there has been too many damned lies told already and I'm going to keep my mouth shut."

Two months later, a jury was selected to sort fact from fiction, and the prisoners were brought back to Glencoe for a chance to tell their side of the story in court. Musgrove, the man who pulled the fatal trigger, was the first man to go on trial. Emotions in the community were still running high. Spectators of the case tried to show restraint, but several hissed and protested when the defense tried to paint a picture of the sheriff's killing being an accident.

In the end, the jury found Musgrove guilty of second-degree murder. It took nine hours to reach this verdict, and due to this ruling, Cingmars was expected to face manslaughter charges at his upcoming trial.

For some, that wasn't good enough.

The verdict made it clear that both criminals would avoid the death penalty, and resentment in the Glencoe community intensified as a result. Lawyers in the case even grew concerned, worried that lingering tensions in the town might spiral out of control. The judge felt differently, confident that Glencoe's citizens would respect the court's decision.

He was wrong.

After Musgrove's trial, the men were transported back to the Glencoe jail to await Cingmars' turn in court. There, the silent rage festering in the community—dark and impatient—finally exploded.

In another twist of irony, what came next had shades of Cingmars' robbery in Morrison. It started around midnight on Saturday, September 5, 1896, when there was a gentle knock on the (jailhouse) door. When the jailer answered, masked men pushed their way inside, one holding a sledgehammer. A mob surrounding the jail flooded in. They demanded the prisoners.

When guards refused, they were either tied up or pushed into a corner.

One of the night watchmen tried to plead with the angry mob, a crowd of roughly thirty men, all dressed in black. "Think over what you are going to do. The day will come when you will regret your actions here tonight. Let the law take its course."

The mob paid this no attention.

They tried using keys to open the cell doors, and when that didn't work, the sledgehammer did.

From there, it appears that Cingmars' last moments were anything but dignified. A jailer later recalled that when Musgrove and Cingmars were awakened by the sounds of the mob thundering toward them, there were no defiant shouts of "well, we don't have to go" this time.

Instead, the men knew a dire fate was at hand and let out pitiful yelps and prayers, begging for mercy. The mob paid this no attention either, gagging their mouths to prevent further commotion.

Next, the prisoners were told to get dressed, and ropes were knotted around their necks.

Far away in Glencoe, Minnesota, hundreds of miles from his past crimes in rural Morrison, Wisconsin, Cingmars understood his days on the run were not only over, but his life would soon be, too. As he was led out of the jail, Cingmars could be heard mumbling pitifully for his "Mother."

Asleep and unaware of these cries in the night, Cingmars' mother was staying elsewhere in Glencoe, awaiting her son's upcoming appearance in court. When informed the next day of what you'll learn about next, she let out wails of grief, tore at her hair, fell to the ground, and rolled on the floor, sobbing.

"My heart is broken. My heart is broken! I do not want to live. My darling boy, oh, my darling boy," she cried in terrible anguish.

Carrying rope and supplies, the mob led Cingmars and Musgrove away into the night. Jailers tried to sound an alarm, but it was no use. The angry mob worked quickly, hanging Cingmars and his fellow outlaw off a bridge near Buffalo Creek.

It was the same bridge Sheriff Rogers had crossed months earlier when he set out to arrest them.

Musgrove fell from one side. Cingmars from the other.

The drop was nearly fifteen feet.

Both men were found with their necks broken and boots hanging lifeless in the water below them.

It was finally over. The lights went out for Cingmars. The crowd that had gathered scattered away like leaves in the wind.

There was nothing left to see.

End of an Era

It's hard to believe that so many odd tales and interesting moments have been tucked away in the Town of Morrison's distant past, right?

As we've explored throughout this book, for anyone who believes nothing exciting ever happens in Morrison, its pioneer history offers a quiet rebuttal.

The Town of Morrison's earliest residents carved out not just farms, schools, and businesses, but a lasting community... and plenty of misadventures and memories along the way.

Their long, difficult journey from wilderness to prosperity was celebrated a century later, on September 18, 1955.

On that cozy Sunday, the Town of Morrison marked its 100th anniversary with a grand centennial celebration. It's estimated that between 10,000 and 15,000 people gathered at the event—a notable feat for a small, unincorporated community. Together, the large crowd honored the sacrifices and achievements of early settlers who transformed the surrounding landscape into a thriving town.

Throughout the day, residents and visitors alike enjoyed a parade that stretched down the town's main roads, showcasing relics from pioneer days. Oxen-drawn wagons, antique buggies, early farm equipment, and historic clothing were proudly displayed. Local businesses took part, building floats that paid tribute to Morrison's past. Bands played, a dance was held, and neighbors reminisced about the town's shared history. It was a day to celebrate not just what had been built, but the spirit of those who built it: their determination, their hardships, and their triumphs.

The descendants of the first settlers also stood side by side with newer residents, honoring the journey that began a hundred years earlier.

Now, more than seventy years have already passed since that centennial celebration, a day that seemed to close the book on Morrison's pioneer era… yet left the story still turning. After all, the work of building a community never truly ends, and Morrison and its people continue to write new chapters. These new stories are woven into the wind. They whisper across fields and drift along the quiet bends of the riverbank. They creak through old barn doors and rumble gently through laughter at town gatherings.

They bring new echoes of love, loss, and triumph.

Perhaps in a faraway future, someone might pause, reflect, and look back on these moments, too, and realize the echoes of yesterday are a timeless heartbeat that connects us… and carries us forward.

Acknowledgements

This book's journey began with an unexpected spark. While skimming through the archives of *The Brillion News*—back when I worked there as an editor and reporter from 2010 to 2015—I came across an old newspaper article. It was a minor note about a man nicknamed "Mossback," who had an eventful day at a Town of Morrison tavern in the late 1800s. Having grown up in Morrison, this silly story caught my eye. It made me think about the eventful days I shared with my own friends and family members in Morrison's bars, barnyards, and backyards over the years.

I took a picture of that article and decided to share it with some of my old Morrison buddies. For them, it brought smirks, laughter, and that same odd feeling—almost like looking into the distant past and a mirror, all at the same time.

That single moment of shared amusement opened the door to a deeper curiosity for me—one that would lead to uncovering more stories and far more history in my old hometown than I ever imagined possible.

Thank you for reading this book, which is the end result of that deep curiosity. It was a fun-filled, surprising journey to research and write *Echoes of Morrison*. I worked on this project off and on in my spare time over the course of several years. The more research that went into this, the more fascinating it became for me, and I hope you found it interesting, too.

I want to thank everyone who shaped not only this book, but the personal memories of Morrison that live within me. Those are not headline-worthy memories that will live on in newspaper clippings or history books, but they have left an indelible mark on my life, and I forever appreciate it.

To my grandparents—Norman, Jean, Lorraine, and Al—thank you for passing down stories, strength, and a way of life that was pulled from your yesterdays and passed on gently with hugs and smiles. And to my grandfather Wilmer, whom I never had the chance to meet, yet whose spirit echoes so clearly through my father and uncles—thank you, too.

Thank you also to other relatives that lived even further back, in the very pioneer years that I've highlighted in the book. These individuals operated farms in the Morrison community and surrounding area for generations. They, too, endured many of the same hardships experienced by others in this book. For example, my great-great-*great* grandfather, Friedrich Pantzlaff—the first family member on my father's side to come to the region from Europe around 1850—was killed on his Cooperstown farm in an accident with his horses. He was 72. Another relative was gored and killed by a bull. In generations to follow, others in my family endured barn fires, injuries, and misfortune while working day after day on their farms. They carried on. The Pantzlaffs and Loppnows kept pushing forward, and I'm grateful.

To my parents, Donald and Nancy: thank you for creating my history, much of which happened within the Town of Morrison. What a wonderful place to grow up, with even more wonderful parents. I'm forever grateful for the life you built and the memories you helped me form. You are the most incredible, loving people I know.

To my sisters, Cathy, Sandy, and Patty: our adventures were the heartbeat of my childhood. I'm grateful to be your brother. It's one of my greatest honors.

My uncles and aunts also played an integral role in my life in Morrison, and beyond. To Lori, Lisa, Linda, Ricky, Randy, Norman, JR, Karen, and Vernon, I have wonderful memories of each of you (and your spouses). I quietly observed your words, your spirit, your humor, and grace, and weaved the best of what I saw into my soul.

The same can be said for my many wonderful (and always entertaining) cousins.

Justin, Keith, Kaleb, Hannah, and Brylie, I'm beyond grateful for all the smiles and meaning you add to our family, too.

To my dear old friends—Brian, Adam, Eric, Crystal, Renee, Sally, Jackie, and Phillip—thank you for being part of the early memories that made Morrison so peaceful, fun, and vibrant to me. You were the pillars of my childhood. And to Ron, Jason F., Jason Z., Jason L., Andy, Tyler, and so many others who helped shape the teenage and adult years: thank you for the laughter, the mischief, and the lasting bonds.

Thank you, D.C., for the smiles and good times.

There are countless others from Morrison—neighbors, classmates, crushes, pastors, teachers, coworkers, bosses, additional family members, and other friends (as well as their parents and siblings)—whose names could fill many more pages. Thank you to every person who has helped shaped my journey.

I would also like to express my sincere gratitude to Amanda from the De Pere Historical Society, as well as McKim and James, for our wonderful conversations about the past. The wealth of local history you preserve, highlight, and cherish is appreciated.

I also extend gratitude to the many community journalists I have worked with over the years, especially Tim, Ian, Aaron, and

Ed, and all other newspaper staff in Ripon and Brillion that I was blessed to work with. This book is a testament to how vital journalism remains. Yes, the national media landscape can feel polarizing at times, but those who document the everyday stories of local towns and cities deserve immense credit. This book would not have been possible without it.

Thank you to Kristin Waller for helping polish this book into its final form. Your tremendous eye for detail is cherished and appreciated. Thank you to Maria Precopio Giddings and Greg Brecht for your thoughtful and skilled work in the early stages of this project.

To Cheryl—thank you for your incredible support in making this book possible. Your belief in me matters more than I can say. I just "kept workin' on Morrison," and I'm so grateful you encouraged me to see it through.

And finally, thank you to my children, Olive and Ezra: Every word, every giggle, and every breath you've taken has built my favorite story, one I am beyond blessed to write with you. You are my loves. My inspiration. My everything. Forever, and always. You are the endless echoes of my soul.

About the Author

Zelo Anderson is a resident of De Pere, Wisconsin, who grew up in the nearby Town of Morrison (where he never got into any trouble). He has won more than 25 writing and journalism awards in his career. Zelo has two children and two silly dogs. When he's not writing, hiking, or photographing his surroundings, Zelo regularly contributes to community-based efforts to promote diversity, respect, inclusion, and mental health.

Bibliography

A vast amount of research and organization went into the creation of this book. Sources for the stories that appear in this book are listed below, in chronological order of their original publishing. Most news articles listed have directly informed the stories in this book, while others were used as general references to better understand the featured time period and community. Most of this research was made possible through Newspapers.com, which is a tremendous resource for exploring all manners of history. Many of the articles below were from the Associated Press and various other news organizations. I also utilized other sources, including various internet news websites, and research available from entities like the De Pere Historical Society. There are many stories in this collection and some of them are quite sensitive and harrowing. I hope I've handled all subject matter with the respect, accuracy, honesty, and compassion that it deserves. If I've missed the mark on any of that, I do apologize. Also, despite noble intentions while trying to decipher a large volume of research, I understand that there may be occasional errors in my work. Any mistakes or omissions are regrettable and unintentional. Finally, while trying to preserve a simple and streamlined format for the reader, it is my hope and intention that I've properly cited all sources appropriately and used pieces of all work fairly and correctly. I will gladly make adjustments should any errors be present.

Below are primary references used to formulate the stories and concepts explored in this book:

Shocking Accident – Mr. Howard killed when load of logs capsized. (1859, February 26). *Manitowoc Daily Tribune*, p. 2. Manitowoc, Wisconsin.

Shooting Cattle – T. Morrissy oxen shot. (1859, October 6). *Manitowoc Herald*, p. 2. Manitowoc, Wisconsin.

An Indian Killed by a Bear. (1859, November 23). *The Daily Milwaukee News*, p. 1. Milwaukee, Wisconsin.

Green, Capt. T. H. (1863, January 9). [Letter regarding Michael Rourke]. *The Manitowoc Pilot*, p. 2. Manitowoc, Wisconsin.

Morrison growth and the beating of Mr. Kuntz. (1865, November 30). *Janesville Weekly Gazette*, p. 4. Janesville, Wisconsin.

Breach of Promise – Briget Ryan and John O'Leary. (1868, February 1). *Green Bay Weekly Gazette*, p. 3. Green Bay, Wisconsin.

Small Damage – Briget Ryan and John O'Leary. (1868, February 7). *The Manitowoc Pilot*, p. 1. Manitowoc, Wisconsin.

Reward – for arrest of person who set Michael Quinn's barn on fire in Morrison. (1868, December 26). *Green Bay Weekly Gazette*, p. 5. Green Bay, Wisconsin.

Sudden Death – Morrison farmer drops dead on Pine Street. (1869, February 6). *Green Bay Weekly Gazette*, p. 5. Green Bay, Wisconsin.

Sad – Mother and newborn die at home. (1869, February 6). *The Daily Milwaukee News*, p. 4. Milwaukee, Wisconsin.

Mr. Joyce's wife and newborn found dead. (1869, February 8). *Janesville Gazette*, p. 1. Janesville, Wisconsin.

Assault and battery in Morrison. (1870, June 4). *Green Bay Weekly Gazette*, p. 3. Green Bay, Wisconsin.

Severe storm. (1870, July 23). *Green Bay Weekly Gazette*, p. 3. Green Bay, Wisconsin.

Child lost and found. (1871, July 22). *The Appleton Crescent*, p. 3. Appleton, Wisconsin.

84-year-old man struggles. (1872, September 19). *Beaver Dam Argus*, p. 2. Beaver Dam, Wisconsin.

A Day with the Old Settlers of Morrison. (1873, June 4). *Green Bay Press-Gazette*, p. 4. Green Bay, Wisconsin.

A Day with the Old Settlers of Morrison. (1873, June 7). *Green Bay Weekly Gazette*, p. 3. Green Bay, Wisconsin.

Altmeyer Mill destroyed by fire. (1873, November 5). *Wisconsin State Journal*, p. 2. Madison, Wisconsin.

Altmeyer Mill destroyed by fire. (1873, November 5). *Madison Wisconsin State Journal*, p. 2. Madison, Wisconsin.

A steam saw-mill was destroyed by fire. (1873, November 8). *Green Bay Weekly Gazette*, p. 1. Green Bay, Wisconsin.

Progress of Wrightstown. (1874, March 19). *Appleton Post*, p. 3. Appleton, Wisconsin.

Wrightstown Correspondence. (1874, March 30). *Green Bay Press-Gazette*, p. 4. Green Bay, Wisconsin.

Wrightstown News. (1874, October 15). *Green Bay Press-Gazette*, p. 4. Green Bay, WI.

The Morrison Scandal – Rev. Harm and Carl Schroeder. (1874, December 17). *Green Bay Press-Gazette*, p. 4. Green Bay, Wisconsin.

The Morrison Scandal – Suit Concluded and Verdict Rendered. (1874, December 19). *Green Bay Weekly Gazette*, p. 4. Green Bay, WI.

Town of Morrison Leadership. (1876, April 6). *Green Bay Press-Gazette*, p. 4. Green Bay, Wisconsin.

Outagamie County Court – In Probate; the estate of Melville B Morrison. (1876, August 10). *Appleton Post*, p. 2. Appleton, Wisconsin.

Young man accidentally shot himself. (1876, September 14). *Sturgeon Bay Door County Advocate*, p. 2. Sturgeon Bay, Wisconsin.

Morrison Notes. (1877, March 22). *The Manitowoc Pilot*, p. 3. Manitowoc, Wisconsin.

A.J. Morrison. (1877, April 27). *Green Bay Weekly Gazette*, p. 4. Green Bay, Wisconsin.

Morrison/Wayside News. (1877, May 17). *The Manitowoc Pilot*, p. 3. Manitowoc, Wisconsin.

Morrison cheese-making association meeting. (1877, May 19). *Green Bay Weekly Gazette*, p. 3. Green Bay, Wisconsin.

Morrison Notes. (1877, August 30). [Pilot/Mulloy/Faulk]. *The Manitowoc Pilot*, p. 3. Manitowoc, WI.

Trial of John Gross, justice of the peace from Morrison. (1877, September 17). *Green Bay Press-Gazette*, p. 4. Green Bay, Wisconsin.

John Gross fraud trial. (1877, September 22). *Green Bay Weekly Gazette*, p. 3. Green Bay, Wisconsin.

Cheese Factory in Morrison. (1878, February 7). *Green Bay Advocate*, p. 3. Green Bay, Wisconsin.

Cheese Making in Morrison. (1878, June 6). *Green Bay Advocate*, p. 3. Green Bay, Wisconsin.

Accident in Morrison – Philip Purr. (1878, August 14). *Green Bay Press-Gazette*, p. 4. Green Bay, Wisconsin.

Cheese Making – update on new cheese company in Morrison. (1878, August 15). *Green Bay Advocate*, p. 3. Green Bay, Wisconsin.

The Insane Man – John Maloney. (1878, November 14). *Green Bay Press-Gazette*, p. 4. Green Bay, Wisconsin.

Madman Killed. (1878, November 16). *Janesville Daily Gazette*, p. 1. Janesville, Wisconsin.

A Lunatic Killed. (1878, November 16). *The Oshkosh Northwestern*, p. 4. Oshkosh, Wisconsin.

Maloney jumps off train on way to asylum. (1878, November 21). *The Manitowoc Pilot*, p. 3. Manitowoc, Wisconsin.

Tragic Death of a Lunatic. (1878, November 21). *Sturgeon Bay Door County Advocate*, p. 2. Sturgeon Bay, Wisconsin.

A Madman on the Rampage. (1878, November 21). *Appleton Post*, p. 3. Appleton, Wisconsin.

Muloney the Madman. (1878, November 23). *Green Bay Weekly Gazette*, p. 3. Green Bay, Wisconsin.

Muloney buried on Sunday. (1878, November 23). *Green Bay Weekly Gazette*, p. 3. Green Bay, Wisconsin.

Neighboring Notes. (1878, November 30). [Correction to an incident reported in the Gazette.] *Green Bay Weekly Gazette*, p. 4. Green Bay, Wisconsin.

Another Mill Burned. (1879, June 5). *Green Bay Advocate*, p. 3. Green Bay, Wisconsin.

Hayes steam saw mill destroyed by fire. (1879, June 5). *The Manitowoc Pilot*, p. 3. Manitowoc, Wisconsin.

Saw and shingle mill owned by August Hease was burned. (1879, June 13). *Iowa County Democrat*, p. 10. Mineral Point, Wisconsin.

Neighboring Notes – Wayside, Morrison 4th of July celebration. (1879, July 1). *Green Bay Press-Gazette*, p. 4. Green Bay, Wisconsin.

Wanted in Morrison. (1880, February 26). *Green Bay Press-Gazette*, p. 4. Green Bay, Wisconsin.

Killed – Julia Pepper struck by lightning. (1880, June 17). *Green Bay Advocate*, p. 3. Green Bay, Wisconsin.

Julia Pepper, seventeen years old, killed by lightning. (1880, June 19) *Green Bay Weekly Gazette*, p. 3. Green Bay, Wisconsin.

Wrightstown News. (1880, July 3). *Green Bay Weekly Gazette*, p. 4. Green Bay, Wisconsin.

Morrison – John Crowley informs on cheese factory. (1880, July 8). *Green Bay Advocate*, p. 3. Green Bay, Wisconsin.

Wayside Notes – Morrison. (1880, July 15). *Green Bay Advocate*, p. 3. Green Bay, Wisconsin.

Morrison Cheese. (1880, October 6). *Green Bay Press-Gazette*, p. 4. Green Bay, Wisconsin.

Dobbin's Electric Soap. (1880, October 7). *Green Bay Advocate*, p. 2. Green Bay, Wisconsin.

Morrisontown value of property. (1881, January 6). *Green Bay Advocate*, p. 4. Green Bay, Wisconsin.

New post office established in town of Morrison. (1881, February 3). *Green Bay Advocate*, p. 3. Green Bay, Wisconsin.

Post office established in town of Morrison. (1881, February 12). *Stevens Point Daily Journal*, p. 2. Stevens Point, Wisconsin.

Morrison town appointments. (1881, April 7). *Green Bay Press-Gazette*, p. 4. Green Bay, Wisconsin.

August Wendorf accidentally shot and killed. (1881, November 8). *Manitowoc Lake Shore Times*, p. 2. Manitowoc, Wisconsin.

News of visitors and deaths. (1882, February 2). *The Manitowoc Pilot*, p. 3. Manitowoc, Wisconsin.

Stephen Leary of Morrisontown brought home dead. (1882, February 23). *The Manitowoc Pilot*, p. 3. Manitowoc, Wisconsin.

Schunk family – two more died from small pox. (1882, March 2). *The Manitowoc Pilot*, p. 3. Manitowoc, Wisconsin.

Horses stolen from stable in town of Morrison. (1882, March 23). *Manitowoc Post*, p. 3. Manitowoc, Wisconsin.

Morrison news. (1882, May 11). *Green Bay Advocate*, p. 3. Green Bay, Wisconsin.

Mr. J. Altmeyer sick with diphtheria. (1882, October 12). *Green Bay Advocate*, (p. 3). Green Bay, Wisconsin.

Cheese and syrup making in Brown County. (1882, November 2). *Green Bay Advocate*, p. 3. Green Bay, Wisconsin.

Considerable business in Wayside, town of Morrison. (1883, January 11). *Green Bay Advocate*, p. 3. Green Bay, Wisconsin.

Morrison – farmers, J. C. Brill, Falck Bros., L. Rockel. (1883, January 11). *Green Bay Advocate*, p. 3. Green Bay, Wisconsin.

Quinsy and mumps flourish in Morrison. (1883, February 13). *Green Bay Press-Gazette*, p. 4. Green Bay, Wisconsin.

N. Altmeyer sold farm of 80 acres. (1883, July 11). *Green Bay Press-Gazette*, p. 4. Green Bay, Wisconsin.

A Singular Freak. (1883, July 14). *Green Bay Weekly Gazette*, p. 4. Green Bay, Wisconsin.

The Storm Elsewhere. (1883, July 26). *Green Bay Advocate*, p. 3. Green Bay, Wisconsin.

East Wrightstown – storm damage. (1883, July 28). *Green Bay Weekly Gazette*, p. 4. Green Bay, Wisconsin.

A new hotel is being erected. (1883, September 4). *Green Bay Press-Gazette*, p. 4. Green Bay, Wisconsin.

Burglaries – house of Philip Falk. (1883, October 5). *Madison Wisconsin State Journal*, p. 1. Madison, Wisconsin.

Burglary – Falck & Bros. (1883, October 6). *Green Bay Weekly Gazette*, p. 4. Green Bay, Wisconsin.

Burglary in Morrison – Falck Brothers. (1883, October 11). *Green Bay Advocate*, p. 3. Green Bay, Wisconsin.

Depere Notes. (1883, December 1). *Green Bay Weekly Gazette*, p. 3. Green Bay, Wisconsin.

Accidental Death – Mr. Philip Snyder. (1884, February 7). *Green Bay Advocate*, p. 3. Green Bay, Wisconsin.

N. Altmeyer says Union House is full all the time. (1884, February 21). *Green Bay Advocate*, p. 3. Green Bay, Wisconsin.

Morrison – considerable building going on in the coming summer. (1884, March 13). *Green Bay Advocate*, p. 3. Green Bay, Wisconsin.

Frank Fresch captures turkey buzzard. (1884, September 2). *Green Bay Press-Gazette*, p. 3. Green Bay, Wisconsin.

Thomas Burke is studying medicine with Dr. Lynch of Morristown. (1884, December 2). *Manitowoc Lake Shore Times*, p. 3. Manitowoc, Wisconsin.

Cattle killed. (1885, February 14). *Green Bay Weekly Gazette*, p. 4. Green Bay, Wisconsin.

Wholesale cattle killing. (1885, February 19). *Green Bay Advocate*, p. 3. Green Bay, Wisconsin.

Lightning passes down chimney of house of Jacob Schunk. (1885, July 11). *Oshkosh Daily Northwestern*, p. 3. Oshkosh, Wisconsin.

More about the Storm. (1885, July 18). *Green Bay Weekly Gazette*, p. 3. Green Bay, Wisconsin.

A Horrible Story. (1885, August 20). *Green Bay Advocate*, p. 3. Green Bay, Wisconsin.

Bones of Contention. (1885, August 22). *Green Bay Weekly Gazette*, p. 4. Green Bay, Wisconsin.

Investigation into Thos. Burke's dissection of human corpse. (1885, September 9). *Oshkosh Daily Northwestern*, p. 3. Oshkosh, Wisconsin.

99-year-old man long walks. (1886, September 23). *De Pere Journal*, p. 2. De Pere, Wisconsin.

James Clark robbed by hired man. (1887, March 19). *The Weekly Wisconsin*, p. 8. Milwaukee, Wisconsin.

Dr. Burke has moved to Wayside. (1887, April 21). *The Manitowoc Pilot*, p. 3. Manitowoc, Wisconsin.

Terrific gale destroys buildings. (1887, May 5). *De Pere Journa*l, p. 1. De Pere, Wisconsin.

Better Than Reported – condition of crops. (1887, July 26). *The Oshkosh Northwestern*, p. 1. Oshkosh, Wisconsin.

Morrisontown woman arrested. (1887, August 18). *The Manitowoc Pilot*, p. 3. Manitowoc, Wisconsin.

Swindlers at Morrison Fair. (1887, October 13). *De Pere Journal*, p. 1. De Pere, Wisconsin.

Hunter shoots deer in Morrison. (1887, October 20). *De Pere Journal*, p. 1. De Pere, Wisconsin.

Man brings watered milk to cheese factory. (1887, October 27). *De Pere Journal*, p. 1. De Pere, Wisconsin.

Obituary – Phillip Falck. (1889, October 8). *Green Bay Press-Gazette*, p. 3. Green Bay, Wisconsin.

5-year-old killed during runaway accident. (1889, October 19) *Sturgeon Bay Door County Advocate*, p. 4. Sturgeon Bay, Wisconsin.

Man loses right arm at Ronk's saw-mill. (1890, April 29) *Green Bay Press-Gazette*, p. 2. Green Bay, Wisconsin.

Morrison man scares girl with pitchfork. (1890, August 14). *De Pere Journal*, p. 5. De Pere, Wisconsin.

Won by Fanny Fern. (1890, August 19). *Green Bay Press-Gazette*, p. 2. Green Bay, Wisconsin.

Boiler Explosion Kills One Man and Seriously Injuring Others. (1891, March 14). *Green Bay Press-Gazette*, p. 3. Green Bay, Wisconsin.

Son of Jerry Brennan killed while playing baseball. (1891, June 8). *The Oshkosh Northwestern*, p. 2. Oshkosh, Wisconsin.

Man works on Yellowstone road. (1891, October 1). De Pere Journal, p. 5. De Pere, Wisconsin.

Effrontery and Theft – Mrs. Jo. Heinrich had cattle stolen. (1892, July 13). *Green Bay Weekly Gazette*, p. 6. Green Bay, Wisconsin.

Burglars attempt to crack the safes of Jacob Falck and John Hahn. (1893, January 4). *Green Bay Weekly Gazette*, p. 3. Green Bay, Wisconsin.

Farmer's arm mangled in a feed-cutter. (1893, March 11) *Sturgeon Bay Door County Democrat*, p. 3. Sturgeon Bay, Wisconsin.

Three men rob cheesemaker on his way home from Wayside. (1893, August 17*). Manitowoc Post*, p. 6. Manitowoc, Wisconsin.

Citizens of Morrison offer $400 reward for capture of three burglars. (1893, August 18). *The Oshkosh Northwestern*, p. 2. Oshkosh, Wisconsin.

James Brennan was arrested upon a charge of stealing cattle. (1893, September 6). *The Watertown News*, p. 3. Watertown, Wisconsin.

John Streibel Seriously Injured in a Runaway Accident. (1893, September 6). *The Oshkosh Northwestern*, p. 3. Oshkosh, Wisconsin.

Brennan Found Guilty. (1893, December 20). *The Watertown News*, p. 6. Watertown, Wisconsin.

News of Maple Grove and Wayside. (1895, March 14). *Manitowoc Post*, p. 3. Manitowoc, Wisconsin.

Cheesemen Swindled. (1895, October 16). *Oshkosh Daily Northwestern*, p. 1. Oshkosh, Wisconsin

Chicago Firm Owes Brown County Factories About $2500. (1895, October 16). *The Oshkosh Northwestern*, p. 1. Oshkosh, Wisconsin.

Insane Man at the Jail. (1895, December 5). *Green Bay Press-Gazette*, p. 1. Green Bay, Wisconsin.

Gossip from Wayside. (1896, January 22). *Green Bay Press-Gazette*, p. 2. Green Bay, Wisconsin.

Notes from Wayside. (1896, February 17). *Green Bay Press-Gazette*, p. 2. Green Bay, Wisconsin.

John Zerke Killed in the Town of Morrison – Richard Leisch Severely Injured. (1896, May 14). *Green Bay Press-Gazette*, p. 5. Green Bay, Wisconsin.

Farmers Feel Encouraged – F. C. Saenger of Lark Reports Business Good in that Vicinity. (1896, June 19). *Green Bay Press-Gazette*, p. 5. Green Bay, Wisconsin.

Shot by tramps. (1896, June 25). *The Rochester Daily Post*, p. 4. Rochester, Minnesota.

Behind the bars. (1896, June 27). *Star Tribune*, p. 9. Minneapolis, Minnesota.

Will Go Back to Waupun – James Brennan. (1896, July 1). *The Daily Telegram*, p. 1. Eau Claire, Wisconsin.

Lost Barn and Grain. (1896, September 2). *Green Bay Weekly Gazette*, p. 1. Green Bay, Wisconsin.

Law and order outraged. (1896, September 7). *Star Tribune*, p. 1. Minneapolis, Minnesota.

Lynched. (1896, September 7). *The Minneapolis Journal*, p. 8. Minneapolis, Minnesota.

Lynched two men. (1896, September 10). *Dodge County Citizen*, p. 1. Beaver Dam, Wisconsin.

Tree falls in cedar swamp. (1897, February 3). Green Bay Weekly Gazette, p. 5. Green Bay, Wisconsin.

August Griepentrog. (1897, July 21). *Green Bay Weekly Gazette*, p. 5. Green Bay, Wisconsin.

News of Greenleaf. (1897, August 30). *Green Bay Press-Gazette*, p. 2. Green Bay, Wisconsin.

Death of John Clark – A Pioneer of Brown County. (1897, November 19). *The Oshkosh Northwestern*, p. 2. Oshkosh, Wisconsin.

Burglars enter home. (1898, January 27). *The Sheboygan Telegram*, p. 4. Sheboygan, Wisconsin.

Running a Large Force. (1898, June 29). *Green Bay Press-Gazette*, p. 6. Green Bay, Wisconsin.

The cheese factory of F. C. Saenger at Lark is now in full blast. (1898, July 6). *Green Bay Weekly Gazette*, p. 5. Green Bay, Wisconsin.

Death of Phillip Falck. (1889, October 13). *De Pere Journal*, p. 1. De Pere, Wisconsin.

Pot of lye kills young girl. (1889, November 21). *De Pere Journal*, p. 1. De Pere, Wisconsin.

News of Literary Society. (1899, February 2). *The Manitowoc Pilot*, p. 2. Manitowoc, Wisconsin.

Debate between school districts No. 1 and 2. (1899, March 9). *The Manitowoc Pilot*, p. 2. Manitowoc, Wisconsin.

Mr. Glover will begin making cheese. (1899, April 13). *The Manitowoc Pilot*, p. 2. Manitowoc, Wisconsin.

Debate topic is Woman Suffrage. (1899, April 20). *The Manitowoc Pilot*, p. 5. Manitowoc, Wisconsin.

W.L.S. successful debate meeting. (1899, May 11). *The Manitowoc Pilot*, p. 5. Manitowoc, Wisconsin.

"Uncle Tom's Cabin" billed to appear at Wayside. (1899, June 22). *The Manitowoc Pilot*, p. 2. Manitowoc, Wisconsin.

Young man swindled out of $250 by lightning rod sharpers. (1899, July 6). *Manitowoc Post*, p. 10. Manitowoc, Wisconsin.

Morrison man swindled out of $250. (1899, July 6). *The Manitowoc Pilot*, p. 5. Manitowoc, Wisconsin.

De Pere Man Said to Have Deserted Family. (1899, July 28). *Green Bay Press-Gazette*, p. 2. Green Bay, Wisconsin.

Altmayer Returns to De Pere. (1899, August 4). *Green Bay Press-Gazette*, p. 1. Green Bay, Wisconsin.

Defeated at Wayside – Wayside Baseball Defeats De Pere. (1899, August 8). *Green Bay Press-Gazette*, p. 2. Green Bay, Wisconsin.

The Wayside Literary Society picnic will be at Long Lake. (1899, August 10). *The Manitowoc Pilot*, p. 2. Manitowoc, Wisconsin.

W.L.S. picnic at Long Lake was a success. (1899, August 24). *The Manitowoc Pilot*, p. 7. Manitowoc, Wisconsin.

Was Adjudged Insane – Thomas Smith. (1899, November 8). *Green Bay Semi-Weekly Gazette*, p. 5. Green Bay, Wisconsin.

Young clerk arrested for using abusive language on the telephone. (1899, November 16). *The Manitowoc Pilot*, p. 5. Manitowoc, Wisconsin.

John Rectur adjudged not to be insane. (1899, November 18). *Green Bay Semi-Weekly Gazette*, p. 3. Green Bay, Wisconsin.

Wildcat shot in Morrison. (1899, November 28). *Green Bay Press-Gazette*, p. 2. Green Bay, Wisconsin.

"The Deacon's Tribulations" will be presented at Wayside. (1899, December 28). *The Manitowoc Pilot*, p. 4. Manitowoc, Wisconsin.

"The Institute" at Wayside was a great success. (1900, January 11). *The Manitowoc Pilot*, p. 7. Manitowoc, Wisconsin.

Notes from Francis Creek. (1900, February 15). *The Manitowoc Pilot*, p. 7. Manitowoc, Wisconsin.

Woman Kicked by Horse. (1900, April 7). *Green Bay Press-Gazette*, p. 7. Green Bay, Wisconsin.

The marriage of Miss Alice Monahan and Dennis Fielding. (1900, June 27). *Green Bay Semi-Weekly Gazette*, p. 4. Green Bay, Wisconsin.

Cooperstown – Literary societies. (1901, January 17). *The Manitowoc Pilot*, p. 8. Manitowoc, Wisconsin.

A Smooth Swindle of Several Farmers. (1901, April 22). *Green Bay Press-Gazette*, p. 5. Green Bay, Wisconsin.

The City in Brief – funeral and marriage. (1902, June 21). *Green Bay Semi-Weekly Gazette*, p. 5. Green Bay, Wisconsin.

Three Brennan Boys Arrested Tuesday. (1902, July 12). *Green Bay Semi-Weekly Gazette*, p. 5. Green Bay, Wisconsin.

Charged With Passing Counterfeit Money. (1903, January 6). *Green Bay Press-Gazette*, p. 3. Green Bay, Wisconsin.

Letter Made Slow Time – Message Mailed at Morrison August 21, 1892, Reached Green Bay April 8, 1903. (1903, April 10). *Green Bay Press-Gazette*, p. 5. Green Bay, Wisconsin.

News of Kasson. (1904, May 26). *The Manitowoc Pilot*, p. 8. Manitowoc, Wisconsin.

Alfred Schultz under arrest. (1904, September 15). *The Oshkosh Northwestern*, p. 4. Oshkosh, Wisconsin.

Windmill recently placed upon the farm of Aug. Griepentrog. (1904, November 17). *The Marshfield News and Wisconsin Hub*, p. 8. Marshfield, Wisconsin.

Farmers meet at Wayside to improve the cheese business standards. (1905, January 26). *The Manitowoc Pilot*, p. 8. Manitowoc, Wisconsin.

James Brennan Held for Dimmock Murder. (1905, September 28). *Green Bay Press-Gazette*, p. 5. Green Bay, WI.

James Brennan, alias John Jones, bound over brutal murder. (1905, September 29). *The Oshkosh Northwestern*, p. 6. Oshkosh, Wisconsin.

Wayside Literary Society popular. (1905, November 22). *De Pere Journal*, p. 8. De Pere, Wisconsin.

James Brennan acquitted at Escanaba. (1906, January 26). *The Oshkosh Northwestern*, p. 4. Oshkosh, Wisconsin.

Acquittal for "Jim" Brennan. (1906, January 26). *Green Bay Press-Gazette*, p. 1. Green Bay, Wisconsin.

Wayside News Doings. (1907, February 21). *Green Bay Press-Gazette*, p. 2. Green Bay, Wisconsin.

The Fielding Matter. (1907, April 25). *The Manitowoc Pilot*, p. 1. Manitowoc, Wisconsin.

Brennan application for estate of James. (1907, May 19). *De Pere Journal*, p. 7. De Pere, Wisconsin.

News of visitors. (1907, October 8). *Green Bay Press-Gazette*, p. 7. Green Bay, Wisconsin.

Basketball game resulted in neither team winning. (1908, January 23). *The Manitowoc Pilot*, p. 8. Manitowoc, Wisconsin.

Note about the Cato-Wayside basketball game. (1908, January 23). *The Manitowoc Pilot*, p.1. Manitowoc, Wisconsin.

Dies From Goring of an Enraged Bovine. (1908, July 1) *Green Bay Semi-Weekly Gazette*, p. 3. Green Bay, Wisconsin.

Alleged Cause of Trouble Between Couple Now Divorced. (1908, July 25). *The Oshkosh Northwestern*, p. 1. Oshkosh, Wisconsin.

Notes from Kellnersville. (1908, October 8). *The Manitowoc Pilot*, p. 8. Manitowoc, Wisconsin.

Stark Cheese Factory Manager Pays Fine. (1909, August 2). *Green Bay Press-Gazette*, p. 1. Green Bay, Wisconsin.

Rabies in Morrison. (1909, August 20). *De Pere Journal*, p. 3. De Pere, Wisconsin.

Grimms and Wayside Literary Society Debate. (1910, March 3). *The Manitowoc Pilot*, p. 8. Manitowoc, Wisconsin.

A. J. Morrison death and obit. (1911, February 24). *De Pere Journal*, p. 3. De Pere, Wisconsin.

Note from Maple Grove. (1912, July 4). *The Manitowoc Pilot*, p. 8. Manitowoc, Wisconsin.

General news of a dance and baseball game. (1912, July 11). *The Manitowoc Pilot*, p. 8. Manitowoc, Wisconsin.

Town of Lark News Notes. (1912, September 17). *Green Bay Press-Gazette*, p. 5. Green Bay, Wisconsin.

De Pere News in Brief. (1914, August 5). *Green Bay Press-Gazette*, p. 5. Green Bay, Wisconsin.

Auto Bandits Escape. (1914, November 24). *The Oshkosh Northwestern*, p. 1. Oshkosh, Wisconsin.

Yeggmen dynamite safe in the store of George Frosch. (1914, December 3). *Wood County Reporter*, p. 2. Grand Rapids, Wisconsin.

The general store of George Frosch was burglarized. (1914, December 3). *The Manitowoc Pilot*, p. 4. Manitowoc, WI.

Fighter Badly Beaten, Not Killed as Report Received Here Said. (1915, March 15). *Green Bay Press-Gazette*, p. 9. Green Bay, Wisconsin.

Notes from Wayside – Cast of "Capt. Racket" at Dreamland Theatre. (1915, March 25). *The Manitowoc Pilot*, p. 8. Manitowoc, WI.

Girl Sent to Jail – Rose Denny drunk and disorderly. (1915, August 13). *Green Bay Semi-Weekly Gazette*, p. 3. Green Bay, Wisconsin.

Nicholas J. Monahan, Candidate for Municipal Judge. (1916, April 3). *Green Bay Press-Gazette*, p. 8. Green Bay, Wisconsin.

Dairy Lawbreaker Is Fined Heavily. (1916, October 11). *Green Bay Press-Gazette*, p. 1. Green Bay, Wisconsin.

Kaiser's Town of Morrison Is Invaded by Loyalists. (1918, April 8). *Green Bay Press-Gazette*, p. 1. Green Bay, Wisconsin.

Town of Morrison Citizens Will Journey to Green Bay for Loyalty Demonstration. (1918, April 15). *Green Bay Press-Gazette*, p. 1. Green Bay, Wisconsin.

The Town of Morrison – Lutheran congregation of Morrison. (1918, April 18). *Green Bay Press-Gazette*, p. 4. Green Bay, Wisconsin.

"We Are Americans" Assert Town of Morrison Visitors. (1918, April 18). *Green Bay Press-Gazette*, p. 1. Green Bay, Wisconsin.

Morrison loyalty in question. (1918, May 14). *Green Bay Press-Gazette*, p. 6. Green Bay, Wisconsin.

The People's Forum – Morrison Officials. (1918, May 14). *Green Bay Press-Gazette*, p. 6. Green Bay, Wisconsin.

Green Bay Farmer Wanted "His Price" – George Lemke. (1918, May 14). *Daily Leader*, p. 1. Grand Rapids, Wisconsin.

The People's Forum – Morrison's Bond Record. (1918, May 17). *Green Bay Press-Gazette*, p. 6. Green Bay, WI.

George Lemke Fought Liberty Loan and Hoarded His Grain. (1918, May 18). *Daily Leader*, p. 1. Grand Rapids, Wisconsin.

Farmer Is Fined $500. (1918, May 18). *The Oshkosh Northwestern*, p. 15. Oshkosh, Wisconsin.

Lark Soldier Is Killed in Action on Foreign Soil. (1919, March 15). *Green Bay Press-Gazette*, p. 9. Green Bay, Wisconsin.

"Haunted House" Breaks Quiet Life of Town of Morrison and Vicinity. (1919, June 25). *Green Bay Press-Gazette*, p. 1. Green Bay, Wisconsin.

"Haunted House" Is Center of Interest. (1919, June 27). *The Post-Crescent*, p. 3. Appleton, Wisconsin.

Defends Daughter – Arthur Haese. (1919, July 8). *The Post-Crescent*, p. 2. Appleton, Wisconsin.

Declares Pastor Acted Unseemly. (1920, May 18). *Wisconsin State Journal*, p. 4. Madison, Wisconsin.

When the Pew and Pulpit Become Embroiled, Lookout! (1920, May 20). *The Sheboygan Press*, p. 1. Sheboygan, Wisconsin.

Lightning Hits Mill – August Haese. (1920, October 14). *Green Bay Press-Gazette*, p. 3. Green Bay, Wisconsin.

Dan Falck, Morrisontown, lost a gold watch 30 years ago; presented with watch found by famer. (1921, March 29). *Lancaster Teller*, p. 2. Lancaster, Wisconsin.

Dr. Thomas Burke Dies at Green Bay. (1921, June 12). *Wisconsin State Journal*, p. 7. Madison, Wisconsin.

Death of Dr. Burke of Wayside mourned by all. (1921, June 13). *Green Bay Press-Gazette*, p. 13. Green Bay, Wisconsin.

Dr. Burke Dies. (1921, June 14). *Chippewa Herald-Telegram*, p. 2. Chippewa Falls, Wisconsin.

Flags at Half Mast During Burke Rites. (1921, June 15). *Green Bay Press-Gazette*, p. 1. Green Bay, Wisconsin.

News from County – Notes from Wayside. (1921, June 23). *Manitowoc Post*, p. 15. Manitowoc, Wisconsin.

News of visitors. (1921, August 11). *The Manitowoc Pilot*, p. 8. Manitowoc, Wisconsin.

Dr. Rapp gives interesting talk. (1921, December 15). *The Manitowoc Pilot*, p. 8. Manitowoc, Wisconsin.

Burke, T. (1922, October 28). The Branch River. *Manitowoc Herald News*, p. 46. Manitowoc, Wisconsin.

Doctor Makes Quiet Exit. (1922, November 9). *The Manitowoc Pilot*, p. 1. Manitowoc, Wisconsin.

War romance shattered when Dr. Rapp deserted his wife and one child. (1922, November 9). *The Manitowoc Pilot*, p. 8. Manitowoc, Wisconsin.

Fugitive Doctor Taken. (1922, December 14). *The Manitowoc Pilot*, p. 1. Manitowoc, Wisconsin.

Dr. Rapp pleaded guilty. (1922, December 21). *The Manitowoc Pilot*, p. 6. Manitowoc, Wisconsin.

Notes from Maple Grove – Dr. Rapp. (1922, December 21). *The Manitowoc Pilot*, p. 8. Manitowoc, Wisconsin.

Morrison Woman Breaks Collarbone in Orchard. (1925, October 12). *Green Bay Press-Gazette*, p. 5. Green Bay, Wisconsin.

Timothy Reidy, Civil War Vet, Morrison, Dead. (1925, November 5). *Green Bay Press-Gazette*, p. 15. Green Bay, Wisconsin.

Timothy Reidy obit. (1925, November 6). *Green Bay Press-Gazette*, p. 2. Green Bay, Wisconsin.

Timothy Reidy, who fought on both sides of the Civil War, is dead. (1925, November 12). *Waunakee Tribune*, p. 6. Waunakee, Wisconsin.

Morrison Items. (1925, November 30). *Green Bay Press-Gazette*, p. 4. Green Bay, Wisconsin.

Mother Keeps Faith with Son Who Died in France. (1926, May 31). *The Capital Times*, p. 8. Madison, WI.

War hero. (1926, June 23). *Green Bay Press-Gazette*, p. 11. Green Bay, Wisconsin.

Arthur Haese has moved his family to Manitowoc. (1926, December 21). *Green Bay Press-Gazette*, p. 5. Green Bay, Wisconsin.

Wayside Items. (1926, December 28). *Green Bay Press-Gazette*, p. 5. Green Bay, Wisconsin.

Three Brown County men fined following raids by state prohibition agents. (1927, November 28). *Manitowoc Herald News*, p. 3. Manitowoc, Wisconsin.

Andrew A. Bornemann, Morrison, Succumbs. (1927, December 22). *Green Bay Press-Gazette*, p. 16. Green Bay, Wisconsin.

Grand Old Lady Recalls Pioneer Days – Susan Altmayer. (1928, September 8). *News-Record*, p. 1. Neenah, Wisconsin.

Mrs. Altmayer Came to De Pere When Wolves Roamed Forests. (1928, September 12). *Green Bay Press-Gazette*, p. 18. Green Bay, Wisconsin.

DePere Woman, Aged 90 Active In Community. (1928, September 17). *The Post-Crescent*, p.12. Appleton, Wisconsin.

Lightning caused a $10,000 loss at farm. (1928, October 6). *Manitowoc Herald News*, p. 3. Manitowoc, Wisconsin.

100 Chickens Lost. (1930, May 2). *Green Bay Press-Gazette*, p. 2. Green Bay, Wisconsin.

Mother of Menasha Man Is Laid to Rest. (1930, June 7). *The Oshkosh Northwestern*, p. 13. Oshkosh, Wisconsin.

Funeral of Timothy Brennan. (1931, September 3). *De Pere Journal*, p. 4. De Pere, Wisconsin.

Wayside State Bank Entered, but Robbers Frightened Away with but Small "Reward." (1931, October 16). *Manitowoc Herald News*, p. 1. Manitowoc, Wisconsin.

First Clues to Job Disclosed There Today. (1931, October 17). *Manitowoc Herald News*, p. 3. Manitowoc, Wisconsin.

Mrs. Marie Rice, 95, died; last survivor of the early pioneers. (1931, October 31). *Sheboygan Press*, p. 12. Sheboygan, Wisconsin.

Mother of Former Priest Dies at Age 95. (1931, November 2). *Manitowoc Herald News*, p. 7. Manitowoc, Wisconsin.

Hurled 60 Feet, Farmer Dies in Dynamite Blast. (1931, November 6). *Madison Capital Times*, p. 4. Madison, Wisconsin.

Wayside News Notes – "Paying the Fiddler" was largely attended. (1931, November 11). *Green Bay Press-Gazette*, p. 4. Green Bay, Wisconsin.

Little Relief Expected Before Friday, Lowest Tonight About -15. (1933, February 9). *Green Bay Press-Gazette*, p. 1. Green Bay, Wisconsin.

Town of Morrison accused of pro-German sympathies [April 18, 1918]. (1934, April 18). *Green Bay Press-Gazette*, p. 20. Green Bay, Wisconsin.

20 Years Ago Today – Bandits blew up a safe in the Wayside post office. (1934, November 24). *Green Bay Press-Gazette*, p. 6. Green Bay, Wisconsin.

Kicked Under Horse's Hoofs – Ferdinand Beimborn. (1935, September 23). *Manitowoc Herald Times*, p. 3. Manitowoc, Wisconsin.

Testifies Chickens Disappear After Visit of Two Bill Collectors. (1935, November 6). *Manitowoc Herald Times*, p. 2. Manitowoc, Wisconsin.

Morrison Church Will Be 75 Years Old This Sunday. (1937, September 10). *Green Bay Press-Gazette*, p. 8. Green Bay, Wisconsin.

An Irish famer "went to town" in a big way. (1938, July 22). *The Manitowoc Sun-Messenger*, p. 1. Manitowoc, Wisconsin.

Bull Attacks, Kills 72-Year-Old Farmer. (1938, August 12). *Appleton Post Crescent*, p. 1. Appleton, Wisconsin.

20 Years Ago Today – Hundreds come to visit "haunted house." (1939, June 26). *Green Bay Press-Gazette*, p. 6. Green Bay, Wisconsin.

Drowns Tuesday – Sarah Keehan. (1939, July 12). *Green Bay Press-Gazette*, p. 8. Green Bay, Wisconsin.

Is Seriously Hurt in Fall – Ladder Collapses. (1939, October 5). *Manitowoc Herald Times*, p. 20. Manitowoc, Wisconsin.

Miss Mary Jane Clark Succumbs in Oshkosh. (1940, January 22). *Green Bay Press-Gazette*, p. 12. Green Bay, Wisconsin.

Arthur Fritch, Stark, cheese factory operator fined for unsanitary conditions. (1940, June 15). *Green Bay Press-Gazette*, p. 5. Green Bay, Wisconsin.

Mysterious deaths of six head of cattle traced to lead poisoning. (1940, July 5). *The Manitowoc Sun-Messenger*, p. 2. Manitowoc, Wisconsin.

Formal Opening of Pfeffer's Bowling Alleys. (1940, September 27). *Green Bay Press-Gazette*, p. 16. Green Bay, Wisconsin.

Poultry Thieves Keep Sheriff's Office Busy. (1940, November 19). *Green Bay Press-Gazette*, p. 6. Green Bay, Wisconsin.

Fred Pingel, 81, former bank president at Wayside, died. (1942, April 14). *Manitowoc Herald Times*, p. 14. Manitowoc, Wisconsin.

Judge Monahan Dies at Green Bay. (1944, March 13). *The Oshkosh Northwestern*, p. 13. Oshkosh, Wisconsin.

Judge Monahan of Green Bay Is Dead. (1944, March 13). *La Crosse Tribune and Leader Press*, p. 9. La Crosse, Wisconsin.

Two Soldiers of County Dead; Toll In War II Now 116. (1945, March 30). *Manitowoc Herald Times*, p. 2. Manitowoc, Wisconsin.

Cheesemakers Are Fined $25, Costs. (1946, July 26). *Green Bay Press-Gazette*, p. 6. Green Bay, Wisconsin.

Auction Sale on [Wayside] Theatre. (1946, September 4). *Green Bay Press-Gazette*, p. 25. Green Bay, Wisconsin.

Crippled man lashed to bed. (1946, November 18). *Two Rivers Reporter*, p. 2. Two Rivers, Wisconsin.

13 Night Spots Near Green Bay Raided by Agents. (1948, February 3). *Rhinelander Daily News*, p. 1. Rhinelander, Wisconsin.

Three tavern operators charged with sale of liquor after hours. (1948, February 3). *Sheboygan Press*, p. 15. Sheboygan, Wisconsin.

Public Sale Wayside Theater Building and Lot. (1948, July 10). *Green Bay Press-Gazette*, p. 21. Green Bay, Wisconsin.

Plead Innocent to Gambling Charges. (1950, May 2). *La Crosse Tribune*, p. 2. Lac Crosse, Wisconsin.

Wounds Wife, Kills Himself. (1950, October 13). *Green Bay Press-Gazette*, p. 1-2. Green Bay, Wisconsin.

State Woman Dies of Shotgun Wound. (1950, October 16). *Wisconsin State Journal*, p. 11. Madison, Wisconsin.

Emigrating Southerners Find Little Hospitality in North. (1951, May 9). *Manitowoc Herald Times*, p. 2. Manitowoc, Wisconsin.

Green Bay Man Fatally Burned In Explosion. (1951, May 21). *Green Bay Press-Gazette*, p. 1. Green Bay, Wisconsin.

Horribly Burned, Man Drives Auto a Mile for Help. (1951, May 21) *Sheboygan Press*, p. 12. Sheboygan, Wisconsin.

Cheese Factory Fire Fatal to New Owner. (1951, May 21). *Monroe Evening Times*, p. 8. Monroe, Wisconsin.

Suit Over Factory Death Is Settled. (1952, March 5). *Green Bay Press-Gazette*, p. 30. Green Bay, Wisconsin.

Irish pioneers settled what eventually became Morrison. (1954, December 23). *Green Bay Press-Gazette*, p. 21. Green Bay, Wisconsin.

Woman Dies By Drowning – Branch River. (1955, August 26). *Green Bay Press-Gazette*, p. 5. Green Bay, Wisconsin.

Mrs. John Kuchenbecker Drowns in Pond. (1955, August 27). *Kenosha Evening News*, p. 1. Kenosha, Wisconsin.

Parade Featuring Many Relics from Pioneer Times Planned at Morrison Centennial Celebration Sunday. (1955, September 14). *Green Bay Press-Gazette*, p. 16. Green Bay, Wisconsin.

Election in 1855 – Morrison first election. (1955, September 14). *Green Bay Press-Gazette*, p. 16. Green Bay, Wisconsin.

Morrison Trading Center. (1955, September 14). *Green Bay Press-Gazette*, p. 16. Green Bay, Wisconsin.

Morrison Will Have Centennial Festival Sunday. (1955, September 14). *Manitowoc Herald Times*, p. 2. Manitowoc, Wisconsin.

Morrison Was Named After a Man Who Was Trained as a Preacher. (1955, September 16). *Green Bay Press-Gazette*, p. 12. Green Bay, Wisconsin.

Centennial Queen – Miss Phyllis Falck. (1955, September 19). *Green Bay Press-Gazette*, p. 26. Green Bay, WI.

House Finds Morrison Village Area Study in History and Americana. (1959, September 18). *The Post-Crescent*, p. 3. Appleton, Wisconsin.

Morrison honors first settler with town name. (1960, April 30). *Green Bay Press-Gazette*, p. 4. Green Bay, Wisconsin.

Wagner, Saenger – History of community. (1960, September 24). *The Post-Crescent*, p. 2. Appleton, Wisconsin.

Brown Co. to Dedicate Way-Morr Park Sunday. (1961, June 8). *Green Bay Press-Gazette*, p. 31. Green Bay, Wisconsin.

Zion Lutheran Church to Observe Centennial. (1962, June 21). *Manitowoc Herald Times*, p. 6. Manitowoc, Wisconsin.

Way-Morr Park improvement. (1962, July 27). *Green Bay Press-Gazette*, p. 3. Green Bay, Wisconsin.

Attorney Thomas Burke Dies at Age of 70. (1967, January 30). *Wisconsin State Journal*, p. 20. Madison, Wisconsin.

Wayside Telephone Company First With Push Button Dialing Phone. (1968, November 28). *Manitowoc Herald Times*, p. 9. Manitowoc, Wisconsin.

Sleet storm. (1968, December 1). *Green Bay Press-Gazette*, p. 37. Green Bay, Wisconsin.

Old tavern now showplace. (1980, January 13). *Green Bay Press-Gazette*, p. 75. Green Bay, Wisconsin.

The Union Hotel: A De Pere tradition for the last 100 years. (1983, July 10). *Green Bay Press-Gazette, p. 61-62*. Green Bay, Wisconsin.

Farmer – 17 local farm families honored at Brown County Fair. (1985, August 18). *Green Bay Press-Gazette*, p. 16. Green Bay, Wisconsin.

The Evolution of Teaching – Retirees reflect on how times change. (1986, September 16). *Green Bay Press-Gazette*, p. 8-9. Green Bay, Wisconsin.

The discipline of Miss Altmayer. (1989, September 17). *The Post-Crescent*, p. 13. Appleton, Wisconsin.

Union Hotel is De Pere's gathering spot. (1990, May 20). *Green Bay Press-Gazette*, p. 234. Green Bay, Wisconsin.

Humans, animals foul drinking water – coliform bacteria contamination. (2006, March 1). *Green Bay Press-Gazette*, p. 6. Green Bay, Wisconsin.

County looking for ways to protect future of wells. (2006, March 31). *The Post-Crescent*, p. 3. Appleton, Wisconsin.

Ordinance Number 06-05 – manure spreading in Morrison. (2006, October 9). *Green Bay Press-Gazette*, p. 12. Green Bay, Wisconsin.

Number of contaminated wells down in Morrison. (2007, March 16). *Green Bay Press-Gazette*, p. 37. Green Bay, Wisconsin.

Human remains open homicide case – Skull and other bones found in Brown County. (2008, November 28). *Green Bay Press-Gazette*, p. 3. Green Bay, Wisconsin.

Wind Turbine Issue Sparks Resident Debate. (2010, June 20). *Green Bay Press-Gazette*, p. 13. Green Bay, Wisconsin.

Man pushes – literally – for wind turbines in southern Brown Co. (2011, January 16). *Green Bay Press-Gazette*, p. 3. Green Bay, Wisconsin.

Wind farms still an issue in Glenmore, Morrison. (2011, March 31). *Green Bay Press-Gazette*, p. 7. Green Bay, Wisconsin.

Group sues over gag on wind turbine signage. (2012, May 30). *The Country Today*, p. A3. Eau Claire, Wisconsin.

Union Hotel rules for 100 years. (2017, September 3). *Kenosha News*, p. 45. Kenosha, Wisconsin.

The following publications were also used for minor cross-referencing, notes, and insight for select chapters in this book.

Wrightstown Remembered. (2010, January 1). R. Roebke-Berens & J. Berens. Hardcover. Strangling angel section, various pages.

De Pere of Yesteryear, Volume II. Milquet, M. K. (Whitbeck) & Milquet, D. (n.d.). Altmeyer section, various pages.

Town of Morrison, 1855–2005. (2005). Propson, R. & Gillett, K. Hardcover. Various sections, various pages.

Various archived articles within the *The Brillion News*, for which I served as a reporter and editor for five years, were also used to supply several facts within this book. Those records were mostly pulled from the years 1890 to 1905.

A short excerpt of Martha Lemke's diary was also shared with me by a family member. I used scenes from that in two small sections of this book.

Below are additional topics and references that do not appear in this book but were used during my research to build a broader understanding of the community during the pioneer era:

Accident – Morrison teamster severely hurt. (1869, January 9). *Green Bay Weekly Gazette*, p. 5. Green Bay, Wisconsin.

Morrison teamster falls from load onto ice. (1869, January 12). *Madison Wisconsin State Journal*, p. 1. Madison, Wisconsin.

Land sales. (1871, August 5). *Green Bay Weekly Gazette*, p. 3. Green Bay, Wisconsin.

Absence of the Treasurer and Consequent Hinderance to Investigation. (1874, April 16). *Green Bay Press-Gazette*, p. 4. Green Bay, Wisconsin.

Treasurer Anton Burkart Files an Appearance. (1874, April 18). *Green Bay Press-Gazette*, p. 4. Green Bay, Wisconsin.

The Committee's Report – City Treasury Deficiency. (1874, May 9). *Green Bay Weekly Gazette*, p. 3. Green Bay, Wisconsin.

Burkart bound for $10,000 regarding embezzlement charge. (1874, May 12). *Wisconsin State Journal*, p. 1. Madison, Wisconsin.

A Trifle Hasty – County Board assumes late City Treasurer of Green Bay owes a balance without an investigation. (1874, May 16). *Green Bay Weekly Gazette*, p. 3. Green Bay, Wisconsin.

Town of Morrison tax rolls – Mr. Burkart. (1874, June 3). *Green Bay Press-Gazette*, p. 4. Green Bay, Wisconsin.

Meeting of the City and County Finance Committees. (1874, June 6). *Green Bay Weekly Gazette*, p. 4. Green Bay, Wisconsin.

N. Altmeyer of Morrison is a surgeon and mends legs. [Note: Altmeyer not sure if related to Susan.] (1877, February 8). *Green Bay Advocate*, p. 3. Green Bay, Wisconsin.

Morrison spelling school. (1877, April 5). *Green Bay Advocate*, p. 3. Green Bay, Wisconsin.

Shocking Death at Depere. (1877, April 26). *Green Bay Advocate*, p. 3. Green Bay, Wisconsin.

Cornelius Fielding, orphan boy, looking for work. (1877, October 20). *Green Bay Weekly Gazette*, p. 4. Green Bay, WI.

Burkart's Discharge – A Loop-Hole for Van Stralen. (1878, June 19). *Green Bay Press-Gazette*, p. 4. Green Bay, Wisconsin.

Falck Brothers cheese factory is a success. (1878, July 25). *Green Bay Advocate*, p. 3. Green Bay, Wisconsin.

Sheriff Arthur Kellogg thrown from buggy. (1879, January 16). *Green Bay Advocate*, p. 3. Green Bay, Wisconsin.

Democrats in Brown County in disagreement over Senate nomination. (1879, October 30). *Sturgeon Bay Door County Advocate*, p. 2. Sturgeon Bay, Wisconsin.

Morrison, Brown Co. election news. (1879, November 13). *The Manitowoc Pilot*, p. 3. Manitowoc, Wisconsin.

Morrison, Brown Co. news/deaths. (1879, December 18). *The Manitowoc Pilot*, p. 3. Manitowoc, Wisconsin.

O'Shea, D. (1880, February 5). School meeting in Morrison a success. *Green Bay Advocate*, p. 3. Green Bay, Wisconsin.

James G. Clark performs at church. (1880, March 4). *Green Bay Advocate*, p. 3. Green Bay, Wisconsin.

A Clean Record – Treasurer of Town of Morrison makes report. (1880, March 13). *Green Bay Weekly Gazette*, p. 3. Green Bay, Wisconsin.

Neighboring Notes – Effects of Friday's storm on town of Morrison. (1880, July 14). *Green Bay Press-Gazette*, p. 4. Green Bay, Wisconsin.

Neighboring Notes – Effects of Friday's storm on town of Morrison. (1880, July 17). *Green Bay Weekly Gazette*, p. 4. Green Bay, Wisconsin.

The cattle fair at Morristown. (1883, August 15). *Green Bay Press-Gazette*, p. 4. Green Bay, Wisconsin.

Kaufmann's harness shop at Falck's corners burned Wednesday night. (1884, February 9). *Green Bay Weekly Gazette*, p. 4. Green Bay, Wisconsin.

Fire at Morrison – Charles Kaufman's house and shop. (1884, February 16). *Green Bay Weekly Gazette*, p. 3. Green Bay, Wisconsin.

Dr. Brett recovers runaway mare. (1884, June 22). *Sunday Advance*, p. 8. Green Bay, Wisconsin.

John Hickey of Morrison paralyzed in Catholic church. (1886, October 6). *Green Bay Press-Gazette*, p. 3. Green Bay, Wisconsin.

Three boys from De Pere charged with drunk and disorderly. (1888, October 22). *Green Bay Press-Gazette*, p. 3. Green Bay, Wisconsin.

Thomas Monahan killed by falling timber. (1891, November 19). *Green Bay Press-Gazette*, p. 4. Green Bay, Wisconsin.

Mrs. Herman Buchholz died after a day's illness. (1894, May 11). *Green Bay Press-Gazette*, p. 3. Green Bay, Wisconsin.

Labored Among the Indians – Death of Father Masschelein. (1895, September 28). *Green Bay Press-Gazette*, p. 1. Green Bay, Wisconsin.

Hurt by Falling from a Wagon – Mrs. Krueger. (1896, July 3). *Green Bay Press-Gazette*, p. 5. Green Bay, Wisconsin.

Henry Gilbert Killed by an Explosion at Wrightstown. (1896, July 8). *Green Bay Weekly Gazette*, p. 1. Green Bay, Wisconsin.

His Appointment Revoked. (1899, August 11). *Green Bay Press-Gazette*, p. 5. Green Bay, Wisconsin.

Furs were no protection against the cold of Tuesday. (1901, March 7). *The Manitowoc Pilot*, p. 1. Manitowoc, Wisconsin.

Died At Wayside – Mrs. Patrick Burke, Mother of County Sheriff Burke, Dies Yesterday Morning of Heart Failure. (1901, July 8). *Green Bay Press-Gazette*, p. 5. Green Bay, Wisconsin.

Brings In A 2,700 Pound Load From Wayside. (1901, September 12). *The Manitowoc Pilot*, p. 1. Manitowoc, Wisconsin.

News of Reedsville. (1901, November 21). *The Manitowoc Pilot*, p. 8. Manitowoc, Wisconsin.

Rumored that Dr. Holte to be Wayside's new doctor. (1902, May 28). *Green Bay Semi-Weekly Gazette*, p. 5. Green Bay, Wisconsin.

Died At Home in Wayside – Patrick Burke, Father of Sheriff Burke, Died Yesterday Morning. (1902, September 9). *Green Bay Press-Gazette*, p. 3. Green Bay, Wisconsin.

August Shallow died after eating pork infected with trichinea. (1902, October 6). *Green Bay Press-Gazette*, p. 3. Green Bay, Wisconsin.

Disastrous Fire at Wayside Early This Morning Results in Heavy Loss. (1903, February 9). *Manitowoc Daily Herald*, p. 1. Manitowoc, Wisconsin.

Fire at Wayside Destroys a Couple of Buildings Monday. (1903, February 12). *The Manitowoc Pilot*, p. 1. Manitowoc, Wisconsin.

Dispute Over Road Line – The case of Albert Schultz. (1903, July 21). *Green Bay Press-Gazette*, p. 7. Green Bay, Wisconsin.

Morrison Woman Leaves Hospital. (1904, December 31). *Green Bay Press-Gazette*, p. 5. Green Bay, Wisconsin.

News of Misses Lizzie Fox and Mamie Linnane. (1905, February 9). *The Manitowoc Pilot*, p. 8. Manitowoc, Wisconsin.

Falcks build addition to summer cottage. (1905, May 26). *Green Bay Press-Gazette*, p. 7. Green Bay, Wisconsin.

Morrison Girl Is Demented. (1905, June 28). *Green Bay Press-Gazette*, p. 5. Green Bay, Wisconsin.

Miss Emma C. Schmitt to the Northern State Hospital for the Insane. (1905, June 29). *The Oshkosh Northwestern*, p. 8. Oshkosh, Wisconsin.

Two-year-old Odys Fielding died after an illness. (1905, October 5). *The Manitowoc Pilot*, p. 8. Manitowoc, Wisconsin.

James Reidy, pioneer settler of Brown County, died. (1905, October 7). *The Oshkosh Northwestern*, p. 9. Oshkosh, Wisconsin.

Business meeting elections for Wayside literary society. (1905, November 30). *The Manitowoc Pilot*, p. 8. Manitowoc, Wisconsin.

Peculiar Accident to Morristown Resident. (1907, January 23). *Green Bay Press-Gazette*, p. 5. Green Bay, Wisconsin.

Adding contest results. (1908, June 11). *The Manitowoc Pilot*, p. 1. Manitowoc, Wisconsin.

Notice to Contractors – Bids for construction of double stone arch bridge. (1908, July 31). *Green Bay Press-Gazette*, p. 7. Green Bay, Wisconsin.

Insane Late in Life – Joseph Swetlik adjudged insane. (1908, November 5). *The Manitowoc Pilot*, p. 1. Manitowoc, Wisconsin.

Woman Asks for Divorce. (1908, November 25). *Wausau Daily Herald*, p. 6. Wausau, Wisconsin.

Charges regarding alleged insane person. (1909, June 24). *The Manitowoc Pilot*, p. 4. Manitowoc, Wisconsin.

Family Returns to Their Home Burned. (1909, August 11). *Green Bay Press-Gazette*, p. 5. Green Bay, Wisconsin.

Morrison Man Is to Build in City. (1911, February 8). *Green Bay Semi-Weekly Gazette*, p. 6. Green Bay, Wisconsin.

Notice to Contractors – Bids to build Wayside State Bank. (1911, July 6). *The Manitowoc Pilot*, p. 4. Manitowoc, Wisconsin.

Dr. James Burke Is Dead at Wayside. (1911, October 13). *Green Bay Press-Gazette*, p. 11. Green Bay, Wisconsin.

Dr. James Burke died at Wayside. (1911, October 19). *The Manitowoc Pilot*, p. 1. Manitowoc, Wisconsin.

Notes from Grimms – Dr. James Burke passed away. (1911, October 19). *The Manitowoc Pilot*, p. 8. Manitowoc, Wisconsin.

Former Merchant of Wayside Passes Away. (1912, January 22). *Green Bay Press-Gazette*, p. 7. Green Bay, Wisconsin.

Notes from Grimms – Mr. Frank Frosch passed away. (1912, January 25). *The Manitowoc Pilot*, p. 8. Manitowoc, Wisconsin.

Suicide at Home – Veteran of the Civil War Takes Own Life. (1912, July 16). *The Oshkosh Northwestern*, p. 9. Oshkosh, Wisconsin.

Blind Veteran Kills Self. (1912, July 24). *Vernon County Censor*, p. 2. Viroqua, Wisconsin.

Morrison basketball team defeated. (1914, February 5). *Green Bay Press-Gazette*, p. 12. Green Bay, Wisconsin.

Morrison Defeated by Askeaton Team. (1914, February 18). *Green Bay Press-Gazette*, p. 5. Green Bay, Wisconsin.

Old Settler to be Buried Wednesday – Patrick Brennan Dies. (1914, May 11). *Green Bay Press-Gazette*, p. 5. Green Bay, Wisconsin.

Accuse an Indian of Stealing Buggy Robes. (1914, November 5). *Green Bay Press-Gazette*, p. 3. Green Bay, Wisconsin.

To Play Morrison. (1915, January 27). *Green Bay Press-Gazette*, p. 11. Green Bay, Wisconsin.

Buys Dodge Car – William Behl. (1915, August 27). *Green Bay Press-Gazette*, p. 12. Green Bay, WI.

Mr. and Mrs. Emil Jacob are visiting Mr. Jacob's parents. (1915, September 25). *Manitowoc Daily Herald*, p. 3. Manitowoc, Wisconsin.

Farmers Own Many Cars. (1915, October 30). *Green Bay Press-Gazette*, p. 10. Green Bay, Wisconsin.

Wayside Players Capture Two Basketball Contests from Opposing Quintets. (1916, March 1). *Green Bay Press-Gazette*, p. 5. Green Bay, Wisconsin.

Wayside Basket Squad Shows Good Season's Record. (1916, April 8). *Green Bay Press-Gazette*, p. 5. Green Bay, Wisconsin.

The President Pro-Tem of Wisconsin Senate – Timothy Burke. (1917, January 10). *The Oshkosh Northwestern*, p. 1. Oshkosh, Wisconsin.

Monahan Services to Be Held Monday. (1922, January 20). *Green Bay Press-Gazette*, p. 16. Green Bay, Wisconsin.

Notes from Wayside – Mrs. James O'Neil, pioneer resident of Morristown, dies at her home. (1922, February 16). *The Manitowoc Pilot*, p. 8. Manitowoc, Wisconsin.

George Frosch Wayside Man Dies Wednesday. (1922, March 30). *Manitowoc Herald News*, p. 1. Manitowoc, Wisconsin.

Town of Morrison Chairman Is Dead – George Frosch. (1922, March 31). *Green Bay Press-Gazette*, p. 15. Green Bay, Wisconsin.

Will Organize Team. (1923, November 17). *Green Bay Press-Gazette*, p. 4. Green Bay, Wisconsin.

Morrison Loses – Basketball team defeated by Maribel. (1923, November 17). *Green Bay Press-Gazette*, p. 4. Green Bay, Wisconsin.

Brown County Builds 30 Bridges This Year. (1923, November 26). *Madison Capital Times*, p. 3. Madison, Wisconsin.

Morrison Women Win – Sledge pounding event. (1924, July 7). *Green Bay Press-Gazette*, p. 11. Green Bay, Wisconsin.

Morrison basketball team defeated by Kellnersville. (1925, March 11). *Green Bay Press-Gazette*, p. 5. Green Bay, Wisconsin.

Dispute Over Cards. (1925, April 1). *The Oshkosh Northwestern*, p. 4. Oshkosh, Wisconsin.

Morrison Fireman to Picnic Aug. 23. (1925, August 10). *Green Bay Press-Gazette*, p. 15. Green Bay, Wisconsin.

Morrison Children to Give Christmas Party. (1925, December 16). *Green Bay Press-Gazette*, p. 16. Green Bay, Wisconsin.

Good Woman Laid to Rest – Mrs. John O'Malley. (1926, July 8). *Portage Daily Register*, p. 2. Portage, Wisconsin.

Griepentrog Funeral Held at Morrison. (1926, October 28). *The Post-Crescent*, p. 19. Appleton, Wisconsin.

New Zions Evangelical Lutheran Church. (1927, October 27). *Green Bay Press-Gazette*, p. 21. Green Bay, WI.

Morrison News – Evergreen Hall. (1928, September 8). *Green Bay Press-Gazette*, p. 4. Green Bay, Wisconsin.

What the Sunday school has meant for me [Testimonials]. (1928, October 16). *Appleton Post Crescent*, p. 10. Appleton, Wisconsin.

Balloon Dance at the Evergreen. (1928, November 10). *Green Bay Press-Gazette*, p. 17. Green Bay, Wisconsin.

Free Ducks and Geese at the Evergreen. (1928, November 24). *Green Bay Press-Gazette*, p. 17. Green Bay, Wisconsin.

Dance at the Evergreen in Morrison. (1929, April 26). *Green Bay Press-Gazette*, p. 27. Green Bay, Wisconsin.

Francis Goffard Held Under $500 Peace Bond. (1929, May 2). *Green Bay Press-Gazette*, p. 19. Green Bay, Wisconsin.

Kuchenbacker Served 3 Years. (1929, September 14). *Green Bay Press-Gazette*, p. 20. Green Bay, Wisconsin.

Local Man's Brother Dies at Morrison – Herman Kitzerow. (1930, May 29). *Manitowoc Herald News*, p. 2. Manitowoc, Wisconsin.

Swamp Fires – William Kane. (1930, September 17). *Manitowoc Herald News*, p. 18. Manitowoc, Wisconsin.

Wm. Kasten Is Dead, Age 81 – pioneer farmer dies of influenza. (1933, January 27). *Manitowoc Herald Times*, p. 20. Manitowoc, WI.

147

Sabel's Barbers Meet Independents Sunday. (1933, September 30). Green Bay Press-Gazette, p. 4. Green Bay, Wisconsin.

De Pere Badgers and Morristown to Clash. (1934, May 12). *Green Bay Press-Gazette*, p. 11. Green Bay, Wisconsin.

Donald Natzke, Seven Months Old Child, Dies. (1934, May 12). *Green Bay Press-Gazette*, p. 18. Green Bay, Wisconsin.

Hold Loppnow Rites at Wayside Sunday. (1934, August 18). *Green Bay Press-Gazette*, p. 16. Green Bay, Wisconsin.

Chickenpox Halts Play at Morrison. (1934, November 8). *Green Bay Press-Gazette*, p. 10. Green Bay, Wisconsin.

Play in Morrison Friday. (1934, November 13). *Green Bay Press-Gazette*, p. 10. Green Bay, Wisconsin.

Wm. Uecker Dies Thursday – heart attack. (1934, December 21). *Manitowoc Herald Times*, p. 7. Manitowoc, Wisconsin.

Harvey Beimborn charge with creating a disturbance at the Evergreen dance hall. (1935, July 26). *Green Bay Press-Gazette*, p. 23. Green Bay, Wisconsin.

First School in 1848. (1935, August 22). *Green Bay Press-Gazette*, p. 10. Green Bay, Wisconsin.

Greenleaf, Morrison Plan Caging Contest. (1936, April 15). *Green Bay Press-Gazette*, p. 13. Green Bay, Wisconsin.

Schools to Present Plays at Morrison. (1936, April 15). *Green Bay Press-Gazette*, p. 16. Green Bay, Wisconsin.

Capacity Crowd at Plays in Morrison. (1936, April 22). *Green Bay Press-Gazette*, p. 10. Green Bay, Wisconsin.

Hunt for Driver of Death Car – Brown County Man Victim of Vampire Driver Near Wayside. (1936, June 13). *Manitowoc Herald Times*, p. 15. Manitowoc, Wisconsin.

Theft of 1926 Chrysler sedan from Evergreen dance hall. (1936, August 9). *Green Bay Press-Gazette*, p. 7. Green Bay, Wisconsin.

Cattle Rustlers Given State Prison Sentence. (1937, October 19). *Manitowoc Herald Times*, p. 1. Manitowoc, Wisconsin.

Denies Charge of Receiving Four Stolen Heifers. (1937, December 2). *Manitowoc Herald Times*, p. 22. Manitowoc, Wisconsin.

Morrison Woman, 93, Succumbs on Monday. (1938, October 12). *Green Bay Press-Gazette*, p. 19. Green Bay, Wisconsin.

Comedy-Farce will be Presented at Wayside. (1938, November 4). *Green Bay Press-Gazette*, p. 19. Green Bay, Wisconsin.

Widow of Oconto Man Buys Wayside Theater. (1939, January 27). *Green Bay Press-Gazette*, p. 16. Green Bay, Wisconsin.

Four generations, two from Denmark and two from Wayside. (1939, April 12). *Green Bay Press-Gazette*, p. 16. Green Bay, Wisconsin.

Stark School Student Has Perfect Attendance – Roger Pahl. (1940, June 18). *Green Bay Press-Gazette*, p. 4. Green Bay, Wisconsin.

Sportsmen's Group to Sponsor Champion Meet. (1940, July 15). *Green Bay Press-Gazette*, p. 11. Green Bay, Wisconsin.

Conduct Rites for Fred Worm on Wednesday. (1940, October 5). *The Sheboygan Press*, p. 2. Sheboygan, Wisconsin.

Immunization Centers In County Continuing. (1946, April 9). *Green Bay Press-Gazette*, p. 17. Green Bay, Wisconsin.

Miss Wuerger Recent Bride. (1946, October 8). *Green Bay Press-Gazette*, p. 21. Green Bay, Wisconsin.

Louis Saenger, 71, of Morrison Passes. (1947, July 25). *Green Bay Press-Gazette*, p. 8. Green Bay, WI.

800 Attend First Clinics in Schools. (1948, March 24). *Green Bay Press-Gazette*, p. 30. Green Bay, Wisconsin.

John G. Altmeyer Accident Victim. (1950, January 26). *Green Bay Press-Gazette*, p. 17. Green Bay, Wisconsin.

Lutheran Synod to Mark 100th Anniversary Here. (1950, May 18). *Manitowoc Herald Times*, p. 33. Manitowoc, Wisconsin.

Funeral Service Held for August Haese, 56. (1951, August 31). *Green Bay Press-Gazette*, p. 8. Green Bay, Wisconsin.

Edmund Burke, Former Resident of Area, Dies. (1951, December 11). *Green Bay Press-Gazette*, p. 36. Green Bay, Wisconsin.

Morrison Man Dies at Christmas Eve Family Party. (1952, December 26). *Green Bay Press-Gazette*, p. 21. Green Bay, Wisconsin.

Drink of Furniture Polish Fatal to Tot. (1956, October 22). *Rhinelander Daily News*, p. 6. Rhinelander, Wisconsin.

Injured in auto accident. (1958, August 4). *Green Bay Press-Gazette*, p. 10. Green Bay, Wisconsin.

Robert Zipperer, 21, died of injuries suffered in auto accident. (1958, September 22). *Stevens Point Daily Journal*, p. 11. Stevens Point, Wisconsin.

Rotary Roses Program Fetes Mrs. Schwarting – Active in De Pere Musical Circles. (1959, December 9). *Green Bay Press-Gazette*, p. 34. Green Bay, Wisconsin.

Morrison Women Rescued Couple. (1961, February 4). *Green Bay Press-Gazette*, p. 15. Green Bay, Wisconsin.

Sheriff Checking Vandalism Cases. (1964, May 18). *Green Bay Press-Gazette*, p. 11. Green Bay, Wisconsin.

www.ingramcontent.com/pod-product-compliance
Lightning Source LLC
Chambersburg PA
CBHW021056130626
46552CB00005B/2138